Enrico Fermi

and the Revolutions of Modern Physics

Owen Gingerich
General Editor

Enrico Fermi

and the Revolutions of Modern Physics

Dan Cooper

Oxford University Press
New York • Oxford

Oxford University Press, Inc., publishes works that further
Oxford University's objective of excellence
in research, scholarship, and education.

Oxford New York
Auckland Cape Town Dar es Salaam Hong Kong Karachi
Kuala Lumpur Madrid Melbourne Mexico City Nairobi
New Delhi Shanghai Taipei Toronto

With offices in
Argentina Austria Brazil Chile Czech Republic France Greece
Guatemala Hungary Italy Japan Poland Portugal Singapore
South Korea Switzerland Thailand Turkey Ukraine Vietnam

Copyright © 1999 by Dan Cooper
Published by Oxford University Press, Inc.,
198 Madison Avenue, New York, New York 10016
www.oup.com

Oxford is a registered trademark of Oxford University Press

Design: Design Oasis
Layout: Leonard Levitsky
Picture research: Lisa Kirchner

Library of Congress Cataloging-in-Publication Data

Cooper, Dan
Enrico Fermi : and the revolutions of modern physics / Dan Cooper
p. cm. — (Oxford portraits in science)
Includes bibliographical references and index.
Summary: A bibliography of the Nobel Prize-winning physicist whose
work led to the discovery of nuclear fission, the basis of nuclear
power and the atom bomb.
ISBN-13: 978-0-19-511762-2
ISBN-10: 0-19-511762-X
1. Fermi, Enrico, 1901–1954.
2. Nuclear physics—History—Juvenile literature.
3. Physicists—Italy—Biography—Juvenile literature.
[1. Fermi, Enrico, 1901–1954. 2. Nuclear physicists.]
I. Fermi, Enrico, 1901–1954. II. Title. III. Series.
QC16.F46C66   1998
539.7'092—dc21   98-34471

9 8 7 6 5 4

Printed in the United States of America
on acid-free paper

On the cover: Enrico Fermi at Los Alamos in 1946.

Inset: Enrico Fermi at the blackboard during one of his lectures.

Frontispiece: Fermi in 1930 as a full professor at the University of Rome.

Contents

*In memory of
Professor David H. Frisch,
my teacher and guide
to the atomic nucleus*

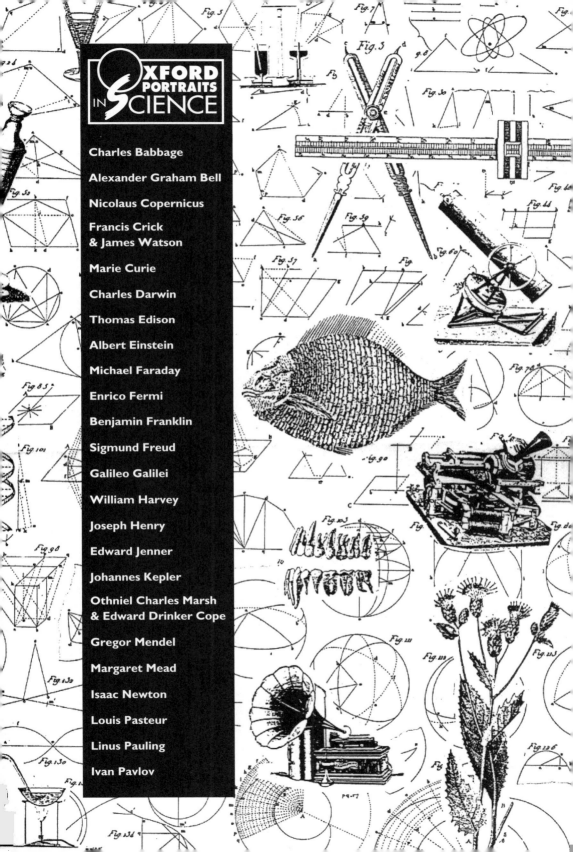

OXFORD PORTRAITS IN SCIENCE

Enrico Fermi (center) at age 4 with his older brother Giulio (left) and sister Maria.

Born in a Revolution

Enrico Fermi was born in the midst of a revolution. No shots were fired, no governments were overthrown, but Fermi's revolution changed the world more than any fought with guns. It was a revolution of ideas and inventions brought on by increased scientific understanding of how the physical world works. That revolution—with Fermi in the forefront—led to the nuclear chain reaction and to the atomic bomb, which has profoundly changed war and put the very future of humanity at risk.

That revolution continues to this day because many questions remain about the ultimate nature of matter and energy. Matter and energy are the concerns of physicists, and Enrico Fermi was, above all else, a physicist. You could argue that he was the greatest physicist of his time.

There are two sorts of physicists. The first kind are experimentalists; they conduct experiments in laboratories to see how the physical world works. Then there are theoretical physicists; they use paper and pencil (or blackboard and chalk or supercomputer) to develop mathematical models and derive equations and "laws" that explain how matter and energy behave. Fermi has been called the "Complete

Sir Godfrey Kneller, the leading portrait painter of his time, produced this first portrait of Sir Isaac Newton in 1689, when Newton was 46. It was not until the dawn of the 20th century, when Fermi was an infant, that scientists revised Newton's theories.

Physicist" because he was a superb experimenter and a brilliant theoretician—a very, very rare combination.

Of course, none of this could have been foreseen when Enrico Fermi was born on September 29, 1901, in Rome, Italy. His father, Alberto, had a secure position as a senior administrator with the Italian railway system. Alberto's father Stefano was the first of the Fermis *not* to be a farmer.

Alberto's education was probably limited to technical high school. Fermi's mother, Ida, was an elementary-school teacher. They married in 1898, and their children were born one right after the other: Maria in 1899, Giulio in 1900, and Enrico a year later. There were no obvious signs of revolution in that middle-class family.

Things were very different in 1901. So much of what we take for granted today simply did not exist. Computers, television, and even radio had not yet been invented. Atomic energy was the stuff of fiction; in fact, the atom was a blurry idea about which there was more debate than knowledge. But that was all about to change . . . a lot. The year 1901, the year in which Fermi was born, can be considered the birth of what is called modern physics, or atomic physics.

With the advantage of hindsight, we can see the peaceful prelude and the gathering forces of revolution. What has come to be called classical physics was thought to be in great shape. Thanks to the work of giants of the past such as Isaac Newton (1642–1727), there was a sound understanding of the laws of motion. Whether it was billiard balls colliding or the planets orbiting around the sun, Newton's laws explained how things moved. Building on the work of the Italian physicist and mathematician Galileo Galilei (1564–1642), the German astronomer Johannes Kepler (1571–1630), and others, Newton had set forth his three great laws of motion:

1. The first law, or law of inertia, states that objects at rest would remain at rest (and objects in motion would continue in motion with no change in speed or direction) unless acted upon by an external force—a push or a pull.
2. The second law says that when force is applied, objects accelerate, their speed increases, and the rate of change of speed is greater, the greater the force applied.
3. The third law asserts that for every action, there is an equal and opposite reaction. For example, a runner's foot presses against the track, and the track presses back on the runner's foot in equal amounts.

Those laws were a source of deep satisfaction for physicists. Combined with Newton's theory of gravitation—the universal force of attraction between all objects—they explained the motion of the planets around the sun. Physicists and astronomers could *measure* the positions of the planets with telescopes. They could compare the measured positions with those predicted by Newton's Laws. Measuring and predicting, predicting and measuring—that was the business of physicists.

It was physics at its best. A few simple laws—and the equations that expressed those laws—explain a wide, wide range of observations. Astronomers could follow the movement of the planets with precision, predict the time of eclipses, and foretell where each planet would be a year from now with mathematical certainty.

Another great triumph of physicists had occurred closer in time to Fermi's birth. The Scottish theoretical physicist James Clerk Maxwell (1831–79) had brought together the theories of electricity and magnetism in a single theory of electromagnetism. Maxwell's equations were as powerful and beautiful as Newton's. What is more, Maxwell's theories of electromagnetism predicted that moving electric charges could produce electromagnetic waves and that those waves moved with the speed of light. Indeed, Maxwell's theories strongly suggested that light itself *was* an electromagnetic wave. (The nature of light had been the subject of dispute for centuries, but experiments by Thomas Young (1773–1829) had confirmed its wavelike properties. Or so it seemed; the revolution eventually upset that applecart too.)

As the 19th century drew to a close, these successes in explaining the physical world led to smug feelings of satisfaction. Some people thought physics would soon be a closed book, with everything understood. But cracks were appearing in this seemingly flawless set of laws. The revolution was gathering force. It would overturn Newton's laws of motion, at least for ultra-small things such as atoms. And light did not always behave like a wave; sometimes it would behave more like a stream of bullets. And there were new wonders—strange new "rays"—in need of new Newtons and Maxwells to explain them.

Nature was slyly revealing some of its true complexity. In Germany in 1895, Wilhelm Conrad Roentgen (1845–1923) had discovered rays that could pass through matter and create an image of the bones in his hand. These penetrating rays seemed to arise when an electric discharge struck the walls of his apparatus. Roentgen called these rays "X rays." We now know that X rays are electromagnetic waves, similar to light but of much higher energy (and therefore better able to penetrate matter).

Roentgen happened onto X rays and their effects by accident, while studying how electricity goes through gases. Physicists had been studying electric currents in gases for fifty or more years. Perhaps there were other laboratories in which the effects of these X rays might have been discovered. But it remained for Roentgen to scratch his head (or maybe it was his beard) and be puzzled by those unexpectedly flourescent spots and penetrating rays, thereby opening an enormous new field of physics. Accidental discoveries have played no small part in experimental physics. (It led to one of Fermi's greatest discoveries and to his Nobel Prize.) Successful researchers learn to explore and exploit those accidents.

The year after Roentgen's discovery, another surprise surfaced—a new set of "rays." In France, Antoine Henri Becquerel (1852–1908) found that certain materials gave off radiation that could darken sealed photo-

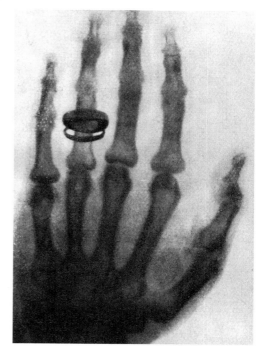

This X-ray of the hand of anatomist Albert von Kölliker was taken on January 23, 1896 at the University of Würzberg, Germany, just weeks after Roentgen's discovery of X-rays at that same institution.

graphic emulsions. This was the completely new phenomenon of *radioactivity*, the ability of some of the heavier elements—such as uranium, thorium, and radium—to emit particles and high-energy X rays. Further investigation led to the identification of three sorts of radiations, labeled alpha, beta, and gamma for the first three letters of the Greek alphabet. Alpha rays (or alpha particles) turned out to be the nuclei, the cores, of helium atoms. Beta rays were the same as electrons, the carriers of electric current. Unlike alpha and beta particles, the gamma rays are electromagnetic wave packets, similar to X rays but with even more energy than most X rays. All of these new findings presented challenges and opportunities to physicists at the dawn of the new century. Something big was happening; suddenly no one felt smug and secure with what Newton and Maxwell had figured out.

There were other discoveries besides those in the laboratories. The physicists who write theories and do mathematical calculations to explain those laboratory results were busy too. These theoretical physicists were grappling with a problem that Maxwell's equations alone could not handle. It concerned the light emitted by objects heated until they were red-hot and glowed. Existing laws led to the impossible conclusion that infinite amounts of energy should be radiated away. The theory also said there would be more and more energy radiated as you went to shorter wavelength, to the blue and violet end of the light spectrum. That made no sense. (They referred to this problem by the colorful name "the ultraviolet catastrophe.")

The German theoretical physicist Max Planck (1858–1947) finally solved this "black-body radiation problem" in the year 1900. The predictions of Planck's new theory were in excellent agreement with the measured amounts and color of the emitted light. To get this agreement, Planck had to introduce the idea of a *quanta*—fixed amounts—of energy. This was no mere technicality. Planck's constant, *h*, which tells the size of the quanta of energy, enabled Planck to make theory and experiment agree.

Even though he did not fully appreciate it himself, Planck's theory was every bit as revolutionary as those puzzling new rays the experimental physicists were discovering. Indeed, Planck's new theory was even more revolutionary, for it provided the first glimmer of understanding of a fundamental aspect of nature. The assumptions built into the theories of Newton and Maxwell were not universal truths. Not all orbits were possible; not all distributions of radiated light were possible. The idea of the quantum was more appropriate to the world of the atom that was already coming fully into view.

Max Planck introduced the concept of quantized energy through his theory of "black-body" radiation.

Changes were coming, too, to the elusive concept of the atom. The word is derived from the Greek *a*, meaning not, and *tom*, meaning cuttable or divisible. The idea that everything was made of atoms, of tiny bits that could not be divided further, had been around for a long, long time, since the days of Democritus, the 4th century B.C. Greek philosopher who first advanced the idea and named the atom. But that was just philosophical speculation unsupported by experiment or theory.

Some insight into the nature of atoms came from the work of chemists, who developed the laws that govern chemical reactions. The English chemist John Dalton (1766–1844) added credibility to the idea of atoms by assigning numbers to indicate relative weights of elements combined in given chemical compounds. While no one knew the weights of individual atoms, the fact that they combined in known proportions helped chemists (and physicists) believe in the underlying idea of atoms.

Dalton had published his work at the beginning of the 19th century, but it was not until a hundred years later, in the early years of the 20th century, that experiments led to our modern picture of the atom. This was a result of experiments in the Manchester, England, laboratory of Ernest Rutherford (1871–1937). Rutherford's experiment consisted of placing a source of alpha particles in front of a small hole and then watching how they are deflected after they strike a thin sheet of gold foil. (One can "see" the deflected alpha particles by having them strike a surface coated with the same sort of fluorescent material that makes a television screen give off light.) Most of Rutherford's alpha particles passed through the foil without substantial change in direction. But a few changed their direction a modest amount, and some changed their direction by a large amount. About 1 in 8,000 was turned through an angle as large as 90 degrees, and some were turned even farther around—almost back to the direction from which they had come.

Now this was a most startling result. It was, Rutherford later wrote, ". . . about as credible as if you had fired a 15-inch shell at a piece of tissue paper and it came back and

Alpha particles, entering from left, are scattered by a thin metal foil. Most alphas are only slightly deflected, but the few that recoil at large angles prove atoms have a dense, central nucleus.

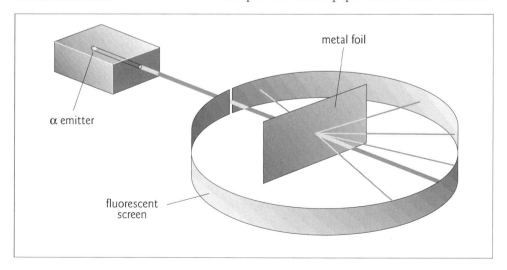

metal foil

α emitter

fluorescent screen

hit you." Here is this fast-moving alpha particle hurtling at that thin gold foil; one would expect it to go clear through and never to be deflected through such a large angle. That incoming alpha particle must have hit something much heavier than itself. Such a result could best be understood if the target gold atoms had their mass concentrated in a small region in the center of each atom. To that region, the heart of the atom, Rutherford gave the name the *nucleus*.

What physicists had, as a new century proceeded, were some puzzling new "rays," a model of the atom with most of its mass concentrated in a central nucleus, and the seed, in Max Planck's idea of the quantum, for a deeper understanding of the nature of the atom. Those revolutions in physics were well underway.

Scientific revolutions do not happen overnight, however. It would be many years before the new discoveries and new theories were fully understood. There would be time enough for young Enrico Fermi to grow up and be a major player in the evolving revolution in physics.

Enrico Fermi at age 17, when he entered the University of Pisa to study for his Ph.D. in physics.

CHAPTER 2

Early Promise
Fulfilled

Maria Fermi was two years older than her brother Enrico, and Giulio was one year older than Enrico. Because the two boys were born so soon after their sister, they were sent to a farm community to live with a wet nurse—a woman who breast-fed them. (In those days, that was not unusual.) Enrico was two and a half before he rejoined his family.

Being so close in age, the three children spent much of their playtime together. Enrico and Giulio were especially close, a bond made even closer by the younger brother's shyness. Mrs. Fermi, a former schoolteacher, had high standards in all matters. She was conscientious—"to a fault"—and expected much of her children. All three children were bright and did well in school. Enrico was regularly at the head of his class without spending all his time studying. Enrico's directness produced few flourishes in composition exercises but was well suited to a "just-the-facts" approach in scientific papers.

In 1908 the Fermis moved, within Rome, to a large apartment building at Via Principe Umberto 133. It was a bare-bones apartment with a toilet but no built-in bathtub, which meant the Fermi children used a portable tub to bathe. There was no heat of any kind, so the children often suffered from the cold. In later years, Fermi told of keeping his hands warm by sitting on them as he studied, turning pages with his tongue to avoid losing the precious heat stored in his hands. It was not an easy life but the sort that builds character and toughness.

Emilio Segrè, longtime student, friend, and colleague, tells, in his biography, *Enrico Fermi, Physicist,* of Fermi's prodigious memory, evidenced by his ability to learn long passages of Italian poetry and recite them many years later. Fermi must have benefited from his good memory and brightness, for he did well in the demanding curriculum at the middle school (*ginnasio,* in Italian) that youngsters entered at age 10. There were many subjects, including Latin, Greek, history, geography, mathematics, physics, natural history, philosophy, and, of course, Italian. And these were difficult courses, taught by demanding teachers. Fermi was, Segrè reports, "easily the best in his class."

Fermi was not a "nerd," or a bookworm, or inclined to spend all his time studying. Fermi was active in sports and very competitive. If it was a hike in the mountains, he wanted to be first to the top. At soccer, he played to win. When swimming, he was the first one into the water, no matter how cold. At least that is the way he was in later years, and that kind of competitiveness is not learned in the library nor much changed with the passage of time.

Fermi was also orderly in his work habits, so he had time left over after his schoolwork for independent reading—especially in science. Even as early as age 10, he later told Segrè, he wrestled with problems in algebra and geometry.

Fermi had a natural bent for mathematics, but physics was his first love. That led him, in his early teens, to use part of his spare time and some of the money saved from his allowance to buy used physics books at the stalls that lined the Roman market called *Campo dei Fiori* (or Field of Flowers).

That interest in math and physics stood Enrico in good stead when tragedy struck the Fermi family in the winter of 1915. Fermi's brother, Giulio, died unexpectedly. Something had gone wrong during what should have been a routine operation to remove an abscess in his throat. Giulio had been Enrico's inseparable best friend. They had played together, built toy electric motors together—things like that. What is more, Giulio had been the livelier, the more outgoing, of the two and thus a shield and guide for his somewhat shy younger brother. It was a great loss for Enrico, a loss that he overcame in part by becoming even more involved in science and science books.

For the boys' mother, it was devastating. Giulio had been her favorite, and now he was gone. Mrs. Fermi became depressed and was never again quite the same. The loss of a child disturbs the natural order of things. It is a terrible blow for any parent, and Ida Fermi was a particularly loving mother.

In this time of loss and great need, Enrico Fermi was fortunate to find a new friend, a schoolmate at the high school, the *liceo*. His name was Enrico too—Enrico Persico—and he shared Fermi's strong interest in physics. They became fast friends, a friendship that lasted a lifetime and led them, years later, to work together on the rejuvenation of Italian physics.

Persico would join Fermi on his trips to the used-book market and would share the books they bought. They also tried some simple experiments together. For example, they found a way to measure the strength of the earth's magnetic field. These two young men also tried to figure out why a spinning top can stay balanced on its tip, but they did not yet have the background to understand the mathematics of tops.

Fermi would soon come to understand why spinning things are stable and a lot more, for he met another helpful influence in his life—a mentor who would help with the important next stage of going off on his own, to college and beyond.

Fermi had begun to meet his father, Alberto, at his railroad office; they would then walk home together. It was a way for them to heal the loss they both felt in the death of Giulio. They were often accompanied by a colleague of Fermi's father, a man named Adolfo Amidei. Unlike Alberto, who had little technical training, Amidei was a university-trained engineer. Knowing that, Enrico began to ask questions and seek answers to fill the many voids in his knowledge of mathematics and physics.

From the first, Amidei could see that Fermi was, as he put it, "a prodigy." Fermi, though only 13 at the time, devoured a book that Amidei lent him, a book on a difficult branch of geometry. In a couple of months, Fermi returned the book, having done all its problems, including many that Amidei had found too difficult. They went on, over the next four years, to books on trigonometry, analytical geometry, calculus, and something called theoretical mechanics. (After this last book, the theory of spinning tops and gyroscopes was well within Enrico's scope.)

Amidei was also struck, as others had been, by Fermi's marvelous memory. For example, when Enrico returned the calculus book, he turned down Amidei's offer to let him keep it, saying he could recall its content as needed. Clearly, this was a remarkably talented person, and Amidei thought hard about where Enrico should go to college.

Of course, there was a fine university right there in Rome. But Amidei argued for the University of Pisa. In Pisa there was also the Scuola Normale Superiore. A Scuola Normale, or Normal School, usually meant a school for training teachers, but the Scuola in Pisa had evolved into something both more and less than that. It was more in that it was now an elite institution, with enrollment limited to about 40 of the best and the brightest in all of Italy, so being

accepted there was a mark of distinction. But it was no longer an institution for training teachers. Rather, the Scuola provided free board and lodging for students enrolled at the University of Pisa, where most classes were held. That was where a person of Fermi's brilliance should study, Amidei reasoned. So Amidei proposed a dual enrollment: Enrico was good enough to go to both the University of Pisa and the Scuola Normale at the same time.

Amidei's reasoning went beyond issues of curriculum. He saw that it would be good for Enrico to get away from his parents' home. Healthy adolescent separation—important in every life—was particularly important in this case because the atmosphere in the Fermi household continued to be mournful and depressing.

The Fermis were not happy. The idea of their one remaining son going off to Pisa for the next four years did not sit well with them. But Amidei and Enrico joined forces and patiently, tactfully helped bring them around.

There was a competitive exam for admission to the Scuola Normale. In a word, Fermi creamed it. Given the subject, "Characteristics of Sound," he responded with an essay that went far beyond what would be expected of a high school graduate. Here was this young man, barely 17, armed with advanced mathematical tools worthy of a person who had a postgraduate degree. The examining professor could hardly believe his eyes. He sought out Fermi to tell him he had never seen the like in all his years and that, of course, Fermi would be accepted at the Scuola with a full scholarship. It was a great boost to Fermi's morale and a great send-off as he left Rome for four very important years in Pisa.

The Scuola was housed in a palace. That may sound great, but old Italian palaces are not luxurious. Once again the living conditions were tough—cold rooms, no hot water. However, Fermi was used to that, and here he was in Pisa, with its Leaning Tower from which the great Galileo had conducted his experiments on falling bodies. That warmed his soul.

Fermi soon found a friend and soul mate, a student at the university named Franco Rasetti. Like Fermi, Rasetti was very interested in science; like Fermi, Rasetti had a prodigious memory. And like Fermi, he was so good at his college studies that there was time left over for hikes in the coastal mountains. A further outlet for their youthful enthusiasm was playing pranks. These pals organized an "anti-neighbor society," devoted to such noble pursuits as mock duels on the rooftops of Pisa. Sometimes they would slip small padlocks through the buttonholes of fellow students who had been distracted by an accomplice.

It was also a good environment for learning still more physics. Fermi and Rasetti soon had the run of the under-graduate laboratory, because the elderly professor in charge could no longer keep up with the rapidly expanding field of modern physics. In fact, he turned the tables and asked Fermi to teach him about the theory of relativity, the revolutionary rethinking of space and time that had been developed by the German theoretical physicist Albert Einstein (1879–1955). Not given to false modesty, Fermi was able to write to his friend Enrico Persico that "At the physics department I am slowly becoming the most influential authority." And it was true; brilliant and largely self-taught, Fermi was powerfully equipped to learn still more physics.

The depth of Fermi's knowledge of physics and mathematics, even after only one year of college, is documented by a notebook he created during the summer of 1919. In it he systematically set forth the theories of mechanics and the structure of matter he had taught himself. He then goes on to treat Planck's revolutionary theory of radiation and other advanced subjects. That notebook is preserved, along with most of Fermi's papers, at the University of Chicago's Joseph Regenstein Library. It shows the clarity of Fermi's thinking and the remarkable range of his learning, even as a college freshman. It also demonstrates his preference for theories that reveal the underlying physics of the subjects being treated. He was not interested in fancy mathematics for its own sake; he wanted to understand what was really going on, how nature itself worked.

Fermi created that notebook from memory. His powerful memory kept things he had learned fresh in his mind, a quality that served him all the days of his life. He also was good at languages and learned German. In those days Germany led in science, and being able to read its scientific journals would be one more advantage for this young man on his way to a distinguished career.

By the fall of 1920—the end of his sophomore year—Fermi had completed all of the standard courses at the University of Pisa and was able to take advantage of a very special opportunity. Because the First World War had depleted the preceding classes of graduate students, there were none who might otherwise have crowded the university's physics research laboratory. Once again, Fermi and Rasetti had free access to the graduate research laboratory as they once had in the teaching lab. While it was less well equipped than a top-notch lab would have been, it was all theirs.

Fermi chose to do experiments with X rays and made that the subject of the dissertation required for his doctoral degree at the university. At first glance, an experimental thesis might seem an odd choice because Fermi had enormous talent as a theoretician. In fact, he had already submitted his first theoretical paper for publication. But Italy had not participated in the great growth in theoretical physics elsewhere in Europe. Fermi simply could not get a degree as a theoretical physicist. No great loss, though, because Fermi was equally at home as an experimentalist, unlike most theoreticians who are ill-suited to the demands of laboratory life. His great competence in both sides of physics strengthened his ability to become a leader in each.

Enrico Fermi received his degree of Doctor of Philosophy in physics from the University of Pisa in July of 1922 and a diploma certifying to his status as a graduate of the Scuola Normale Superiore at the same time. Fermi returned to Rome to rejoin his family and build connections to the physics and mathematics communities in Italy's capital.

He was 21 and eager to put his great knowledge of physics to work at a leading university. But opportunities were few and far between. Even though Fermi's brilliance was widely recognized, there just were no openings. Openings came only when a new post was created or when a professor died and a competition was held to fill the post. Fermi knew that winning one of those competitions depended on having a record of published scientific papers, and he already had six fine papers to his credit. But there simply were no open professorships.

There was an alternative, however. There is a great tradition in science of postdoctoral studies abroad. It is a fine way to broaden one's acquaintance with other scientists and to learn how things are done at the universities of another country. Fermi handily won the competition for the one such fellowship available in the year of his graduation, and he used it to study at the University of Göttingen in Germany during the winter of 1922–23. There the great physicist Max Born (1882–1970) had built a center for theoretical physics that attracted brilliant postdoctoral students from abroad. Fermi was brilliant; he knew German and spoke it well; Born and his wife were friendly. Yet somehow they did not click professionally, or perhaps it was Fermi's shyness and reserved nature that was his undoing. Or it may have been the presence in Göttingen of other brilliant young theoretical physicists, at least two of whom were writing papers with Professor Born. Fermi wrote some papers, too, but on his own. In any event, it seems that he failed to fully exploit the opportunities of this year abroad.

October 1922 marked a profound governmental change in Italy. The Fascists, led by their dictator Benito Mussolini, marched on Rome and took over the government. Fermi recognized from the start that this change was not good for democracy or for science in Italy. Ultimately, it led him to leave the land of his birth, but a long road lay ahead.

In the meantime, the seeds of a happier career move than Göttingen had already been planted. Fermi had made a point of getting to know Orso Mario Corbino, who was the head of the Institute of Physics at the University of Rome. They had met several times before Fermi went to Germany, and Corbino had been very impressed. When Fermi returned from Göttingen, Corbino was able to

Orso Mario Corbino, experimental physicist and Fermi's mentor. Corbino had great faith in Fermi and helped him to secure a position at the University of Rome.

arrange for Fermi to teach a couple of physics courses at the University of Rome for the academic year 1923–24. Also in 1924, both of Fermi's parents died. Though they did not see the full flowering of his accomplishments to come, they had ample reason to be proud of him.

That was followed by another fellowship, this time in Holland, at the University of Leyden in the fall of 1924, under the Dutch physicist Paul Ehrenfest (1880–1933). This fellowship went well. Fermi's interest in what is called statistical mechanics stems from this period and eventually flourished in what is known as Fermi-Dirac statistics, which is discussed later in this chapter. Ehrenfest appreciated Fermi's special talents, and his praise was an important boost for a young postdoctoral student still at the beginning of his career. Ehrenfest knew most of the theoreticians in Europe, and his praise was meaningful.

When Fermi returned to Rome at the end of 1924, there was a university post available to him. Corbino, who was a master of Italian university politics, was able to convince his colleagues at the other universities to have Fermi appointed to an interim post at the University of Florence. The great thing about Florence was that Rasetti, Fermi's friend and colleague from Pisa, was already on the faculty there.

Fermi and Rasetti made a great team. They could share ideas for experiments and discuss the articles in the latest physics journals from abroad. Fermi took the lead when it came to discussing theory, while Rasetti was able to refine Fermi's experimental technique using his own strong instincts as a creative experimenter.

The laboratory in Florence was new but poorly equipped, and the research budget was practically zero. Nonetheless, the two friends carried out a novel experiment that demonstrated how talented they were. They measured

how a varying magnetic field would affect the light emitted by a mercury vapor lamp—that is a lamp that generates light by passing an electric current through a gas made up of mercury. (Many modern highway lights are descendants of those early laboratory tools.) Similar experiments had been done with steady magnetic fields, but it was Fermi who recognized that using a varying field would give new insight into what went on when atoms were in magnetic fields. Light is emitted when mercury atoms, excited by the passage of that electric current, return to their normal or "ground" state.

Fermi easily calculated that a varying magnetic fields of radio waves at a frequency of 1–5 million cycles per second (1–5 megahertz) would be absorbed and produce measurable changes in the emitted light. They scrounged up some vacuum tubes and hand-wound the coils that were also needed to produce electromagnetic waves of the desired frequencies. The experiment worked the first time out—a considerable accomplishment given the marginal nature of their equipment and their lack of previous experience with

Fermi (far right) with Franco Rasetti (left) and Nello Carrara on a mountain-climbing expedition in the 1920s. Fermi was an avid hiker all his life.

radio waves. This was a completely new experimental technique, one that opened the new field now known as radiofrequency spectroscopy—the study of atoms and molecules by means of the radio waves they absorb. Others might have built an entire career on that interesting start. For Fermi and Rasetti, it was another paper, a nice bit of physics, and another step toward getting a permanent academic appointment.

In 1925 there was a competition for a professorship at a minor university. Fermi lost out to an older candidate. But that disappointment did not stop him. Shortly thereafter he wrote his most important theoretical paper, one that put him firmly on the list of world-renowned physicists. It was work that has come to be known as Fermi-Dirac statistics. (Paul Dirac [1902–84] was a very creative British physicist who came up with a similar theory shortly after Fermi did.) This was just the first of many important concepts that bear Fermi's name.

Finally, a breakthrough came in 1926. Convinced that the prejudice against theoretical physics at Italian universities was harming Italy's future, Corbino broke the logjam. A competition was held for a chair of theoretical physics at the University of Rome. Competitors included Fermi's high-school classmate, Enrico Persico, but the 26-year-old Fermi won hands down. As the official notice said, "Fermi, even at his young age and after very few years of scientific activity, already highly honors Italian physics."

Fermi would now return to Rome, rejoin his friends and sister, and more than fulfill that promise. Great things lay ahead.

FERMI-DIRAC STATISTICS: HELPING EXPLAIN THE WORLD

ermi-Dirac statistics concerns the way in which to calculate the properties of a group of particles such as electrons, neutron, or protons. Those particles are called fermions in recognition of Fermi's pioneering role in writing the theory of their group behavior. A physicist might also refer to them as "particles of spin 1/2." The idea of spin arose in early models of the atom, which envisioned electrons orbiting around a nucleus and spinning like a top at the same time. Things being restricted to only certain values in quantum mechanics, the spin of these particles could only be 1/2, 3/2, 5/2, etc. The restrictions were first noted by the Austrian physicist Wolfgang Pauli (1900–58). According to Pauli's "exclusion principle," no two fermions can have the same quantum numbers; in a sense, they cannot be in the same place at the same time.

Wolfgang Pauli, the Austrian-Swiss physicist and creator of the "exclusion principle" that bears his name. It says, in essence, that no two fermions can be in the same quantum state (and thus have the same quantum number).

This seemingly simple idea explains much of how the physical world works. For example, it explains how in going from helium to lithium in the periodic table, that third electron orbiting around the lithium nucleus must be off by itself, making lithium very active chemically, while helium is a very inert, noble gas. Fermi statistics explain ever so much more: how metals and semiconductors conduct electricity, why some substances are hard, even the workings of neutron stars and other astronomical entities.

Incidentally, the other sort of particles, those with spin equal to zero, one, two, or any other integer (photons, the particles of light, are one example), obey what is called Bose-Einstein statistics and are called bosons. Here, the Pauli exclusion principle does not apply, and many photons can be in the same state at the same time. That in turn is what makes lasers possible.

CHAPTER 3

The Road to a Nobel Prize

Fermi was now a professor. That meant he had *tenure*—the position was his for life. With that security, Fermi could start on the large goal he had set for himself: to revolution-ize physics in Italy. He would bring the revolution in physics, already underway elsewhere in Europe, into the classrooms and research laboratories of his native country. That was the task he and his mentor, Professor Corbino, knew had to be done if Italy was to be a serious participant in the development of modern physics.

Corbino had grasped that Fermi was the right person for this tough job. Fermi was a brilliant physicist, well-schooled in classical physics—the theories of mechan-ics and electromagnetism that had been so carefully refined in the preceding century. And Fermi had not stopped there; he had kept up with the most recent developments. He had religiously read the scientific journals from Germany and England containing the latest puzzles and the most recent understanding of modern physics. Fermi wanted Italy to be where the action was: in X-rays, radioactivity, and the physics of the atom and its nucleus. On the theoretical side, there was quantum mechanics—those new theories so dif-

ico and Laura Fermi in their bright-yellow Peugeot. Fermi thought he could afford a car or a wife but not both; Laura proved him wrong.

ferent from the classical mechanics of Newton and Italy's own Galileo. Many of the older physicists in Italy—and elsewhere—resisted quantum mechanics, as older people in every field are likely to resist the new, the revolutionary. Not so for young Fermi; he embraced the new theories, even if he himself sometimes found them puzzling.

Quantum mechanics governs the behavior of the smallest units of matter—atoms and their nuclei. It is a strange realm in which our everyday experience with objects and how they move must be set aside because it no longer applies. In the atomic realm, we must abandon the certainties of Newtonian theories of forces and motion. Newton's laws serve well to explain the motion of large objects—everything from a baseball and bat to our moon orbiting the Earth—but they simply do not fit the way nature behaves when it comes to atoms and their constituents. What experiments showed was that particles (such as electrons) sometimes behaved like waves, and light waves sometimes behaved like particles. For example, the electron, which scientists were used to picturing as a particle, a tiny chunk of matter, could exhibit the properties of waves, producing "interference" patterns similar to those observed with light waves. The classic demonstration of such interference patterns in the case of light waves was the simple experiment first conducted by Thomas Young (1773–1829), an English physician and physicist. Light from a source passes first through a single slit and then through a pair of slits, side by side and parallel to the first slit. The light then strikes a screen. What one sees on the screen is a pattern of bright "lines" separated by dark spaces.

What causes this phenomenon? In the bright regions, the crests of light waves emerging from the two slits are interfering constructively, adding to each other. In the dark regions, crests from from one combine with troughs from the other and the interference is destructive.

The same phenomena have been observed with electrons, neutrons, and other particles, demonstrating their wavelike nature. But light is a wave, and electrons were thought to be particles. Quantum mechanics says they can each be both. Even open-minded Corbino found it hard to accept the quirky quantum theories needed to explain such duality in the world of the atom.

Overcoming those resistances—making quantum theory respectable in the eyes of the older generation and teaching its wonders to a new generation of physicists—was high on the list of tasks before Fermi. Modern physics had to become part of the curriculum, part of the research effort, part of the scene in Italy as it was in other countries of Europe.

Fermi—with his mentor Corbino looking on approvingly—began a three-pronged approach. First, he wanted to convince at least a few graduate students at the University of Rome to learn modern physics. Second, he wanted to start a program of experiments and research in the new physics. And third, he wanted to propagandize for the revolution: to give popular lectures, write articles, and do one further thing that was new in Italy: write a textbook on modern, atomic physics.

Fermi tackled the textbook issue head-on. He devoted his first summer as a professor to writing that book, a slim volume entitled *Introduzione alla fisica atomica* (Introduction to Atomic Physics). His friend and biographer, Emilio Segrè, admiringly records how Fermi went about writing the book: Lying on his back at his vacation spot in the Dolomite mountains in northeastern Italy, Fermi wrote from his deep knowledge and excellent memory. He wrote flawlessly, using pencils, but "there are no erasers on Italian pencils" Segrè points out. The textbook was published the next year.

Recruiting graduate students proved more difficult. Corbino spread the word among his own engineering students. Only one of them came over to study under Fermi, but he was very special. That early student was Eduardo

ENRICO FERMI
PROFESSORE DI FISICA TEORICA NELLA R. UNIVERSITÀ DI ROMA

INTRODUZIONE

ALLA

FISICA ATOMICA

LABORAVI·FIDENTER

BOLOGNA
NICOLA ZANICHELLI
MCMXXVIII

Amaldi, who had met Fermi previously through his father, a leading Italian mathematician. In addition, young Emilio Segrè, who had heard Fermi lecture a few years before and learned more about his work through mutual friends, asked to leave engineering and study physics under Fermi. Corbino—ever the effective administrator—cut through the red tape to make it happen. Both Amaldi and Segrè would stay with Fermi, join him in his research, and eventually become professors in their own right.

Fermi knew the man he wanted to start building a program of experiments in atomic physics. It was Franco Rasetti, his friend from their student days in Pisa. They had also worked together as postgraduate researchers in

Florence, but Rasetti had stayed behind when Fermi moved on to Rome.

Once again Corbino attended to the politics; early in 1927, he arranged for Rasetti to be appointed as his personal assistant in Rome. It was a good choice—there was great camaraderie between Fermi and Rasetti and an important intellectual partnership as well. Just as before, Fermi could deepen Rasetti's understanding of the new quantum theories of the atom, while Rasetti could continue to bring Fermi into flower as an experimentalist.

With teachers Fermi and Rasetti and students Amaldi and Segrè, the beginnings of a modern-physics group had been assembled. Still others soon joined—from the classes in electricity and modern physics that Fermi taught. Each week Fermi held an informal seminar in his office. Seminars are a great way for professors to pass along their learning and style of thinking, and Fermi was gifted in this.

There was no fixed seminar program. Instead, someone usually had a question about a topic of interest. Whatever the subject, Fermi was able to speak clearly about it, drawing on his wide knowledge of physics. Often Fermi would share the work he was doing. Employing what Segrè has called "the eloquence of example," Fermi built up in his students an enthusiasm for physics and a willingness to work hard to be like him. It is sometimes said that graduate students are an extension of their professor's personality, and the growing Fermi school had a particularly inspiring model.

It was not all work, however. Fermi and Rasetti kept up their love of hiking and competitive sports. Both bought cars. Fermi's was a tiny, bright-yellow convertible Peugeot that looked like something out of an old-time comic strip. Fermi would spare no effort to keep his car—dubbed "The Bébé Peugeot"—running. It broke down regularly, giving Fermi many opportunities to demonstrate his experimental ingenuity. (On one occasion, Fermi used the belt from his trousers to replace a broken fan belt.)

The two pals and their friends would drive into the countryside around Rome. One of the group was Laura Capon, a student of science at the University of Rome. Laura was 16 and Enrico 24 when they first met—on a spring Sunday in 1924. He joined a group of her friends and rode a streetcar to what was then countryside, at the confluence of the Aniene and Tiber rivers outside Rome. Fermi took over from the outset, showing an easy self-reliance, a ready smile, and spontaneity that she found attractive.

They played soccer, with Laura, a complete novice, assigned by Fermi to the job of goalkeeper on his team. She saved the day and won the game for them after Fermi stumbled and fell because of a broken shoe. In her memoir, *Atoms in the Family*, Laura Fermi says, "That was the first afternoon I spent with Enrico Fermi and the only instance in which I did better than he."

It was to be more than two years before they met again, this time in July of 1926 at a vacation spot in the Dolomite mountains. Laura's parents were vacationing there, and Fermi came for the summer before taking on his new job as professor in Rome. Once again Fermi took the lead, organizing hikes in the surrounding mountains. "At first sight he gained my [Laura's] mother's confidence, and I . . . was permitted to go on excursions planned by him," she writes. (Clearly, the constraints on the activities of a young woman of 19 were more severe then.)

Things progressed from there, with many meetings at friends' homes after Fermi was established in Rome. Even though Laura had planned to follow a career and not marry, and even though Enrico had described his specifications for a wife in terms that Laura did not meet, and even though Fermi had said he could afford the Peugeot or a wife but not both, love worked its magic. He got both—the girl and the car. Indeed, the little car helped Fermi in courting her, and she became Mrs. Fermi on July 19, 1928. Professor

Fermi was late for his wedding: the sleeves of his new suit were three inches too long, and he needed to fold and sew them to size.

Fermi (center foreground) at his 1928 wedding to Laura Capon (with flowers). The naval officer is her father; to his immediate left is Mario Orso Corbino, Fermi's best man.

The Fermi's had two children, a daughter, Nella, born in January 1931, and a son, Giulio, born in February 1936. Family photographs show Fermi holding the infant Nella rather gingerly; it seems clear that the certainty with which he approached a physics experiment was not matched by his confidence as a young father.

Fermi's first love was for physics and sharing what he knew in seminars. A frequent subject at the seminars was the new wave mechanics, a way of explaining quantum theory that had been published by the Austrian physicist Erwin Schrödinger (1887–1961) only the year before Fermi's arrival in Rome.

Schrödinger had formulated a mathematical way to express the underlying idea of quantum theory, that the location and the speed of an atom could not be determined with the certainty that Newton had assumed in writing

Erwin Schrödinger, the Austrian theoretical physicist, around 1933. Schrödinger developed his wave-mechanics equation to describe motion at the atomic level.

about orbiting planets. In the world of the very small, a different approach is required. Schrödinger postulated a *wave function* that expressed the probability of a particle being at any particular location. It was not easy for those brought up on classical physics to accept, but it worked—it gave the right answers when applied to simple physical situations such as the hydrogen atom with its single electron orbiting around a nucleus consisting of a single, positively charged proton. Fermi liked Schrödinger's way. Ever energetic, he quickly published several papers that were extensions and applications of wave mechanics.

Fermi always wanted the physics to be in evidence. The physicist Hans Bethe, who had spent time with Fermi in ermi had difficulty with the less physical, more mathematical matrix mechanics approach to quantum theory of Werner Heisenberg (1901–76). A matrix is a mathematical entity in the form of a rectanglar array of numbers or symbols. Matrices were introduced into mathematics in the 19th century as a convenient way to express what happens in what is called a linear transformation, when new coordinates x' and y' are derived from x and y. Thus:

$$x' = a_{11}x + a_{12}y$$
$$y' = a_{21}x + a_{22}y$$

Those coefficients form the matrix elements of the matrix **A**:

$$\mathbf{A} = \begin{pmatrix} a_{11} & a_{12} \\ a_{21} & a_{22} \end{pmatrix}$$

Imagine a further transformation that maps x' and y' into x" and y". A matrix that did that might be called **B**:

$$\mathbf{B} = \begin{pmatrix} b_{11} & b_{12} \\ b_{21} & b_{22} \end{pmatrix}$$

Without going into detail, one can define a matrix **C** that represents **A** followed by **B**: **C** = **AB**. It turns out that **AB** ≠ **BA** and Heisenberg used that very fact of "noncommutation" as a way to express the underlying "uncertainty" idea in quantum mechanics that speed and position could not both be determined precisely. This idea plus Newtonian mechanics in matrix form led to quantum mechanics. It was all very formal, very mathematical, but also very profound . . . just the expression of classical laws in matrix form led to quantum mechanics. Fermi preferred the probability approach of Schrödinger's wave mechanics.

Rome and knew him very well when both emigrated to America, wrote in a tribute that Fermi "stripped [a problem] of mathematical complications and of unnecessary formalism" to lay bare and solve the essential physics of the situation. That ability to keep his focus on what was going on rather than on the math is in contrast to the practice of many theoreticians. They use a more formal, less intuitive approach. They prefer to write down equations that describe the problem at hand, solve those equations, and only then begin to think about the physics contained in that solution. So the math comes before the physics for that school. There are whole textbooks and courses with titles such as "Methods of Theoretical Physics" that teach this approach. It has its place . . . an important place. But it was not the approach Fermi liked. He could do the math—indeed he was very good at it. But his special genius was to get at the physics, even at the risk of oversimplifying and obtaining a less exact answer. Fermi was practical, pragmatic. And generations of physicists are grateful for the insights his direct approach provided them.

But Fermi was looking for something more than his personal success—already guaranteed by his accomplishments to that date. He wanted to build a school of physics, to have Italy assume its rightful place among the nations. That meant strengthening the research capabilities of the Institute of Physics, the University of Rome's physics department. And that in turn suggested that he send his associates abroad to learn from more advanced laboratories. Rasetti went to the California Institute of Technology in Pasadena to work with Robert Millikan (1868–1953), who had won the 1923 Nobel Prize in physics for measuring the electric charge on the electron—a very fundamental quantity in atomic physics. Rasetti then went on to learn the techniques for studying radioactivity in Berlin with the physicist Lise Meitner (1878–1968). (This experience proved to be very significant for the Fermi group, which soon needed expertise in radioactivity.)

Segrè and Amaldi were similarly dispatched to European laboratories where they extended their knowledge of advanced techniques in studying light and X rays. Fermi himself spent the summer of 1930 lecturing at the University of Michigan in Ann Arbor—his first visit to America. (Fermi's English—gained from reading British and American journals and from conversations with English-speaking visitors to Rome—served him well in the lectures he gave. Indeed, he was invited to return in 1935.)

The process worked. The reputation of Rome and the Romans grew as did their international network of friends. And, starting in the 1930s, theoretical physicists of the first rank found it useful to visit with Fermi. The stage was set for some big developments that would carry Fermi to the top—a Nobel Prize in physics.

But before all that glory—and the hard work that led to it—there came a small bump in the road. It concerned a paper Fermi submitted to the editors of the great British scientific journal *Nature*. Such editors are gatekeepers of ideas. They decide, with the help of consultant experts, what gets published and what does not. In 1933 Fermi developed a theory that explained beta decay—what happens when a nucleus emits a beta particle, an electron. For his explanation, Fermi had to invent a new, neutral particle, the neutrino (Italian for "little neutral one"). Now that was a very bold idea, but necessary if he was to explain why the emitted electrons were not all of the same energy, but rather showed a characteristic distribution with electrons of many different energies. Total energy could be conserved because the neutrino carried off any energy that did not go to the electrons. (The conservation of energy is a very fundamental feature of all theories in physics, and Fermi would sooner introduce his neutrino than abandon energy conservation.)

He submitted his paper to *Nature*. But the editor turned it down as being "crazy." (He used more polite language—he said it contained "abstract speculations too remote from physical reality," which is a polite way to call an idea crazy.) Fermi recovered and published the theory of beta decay elsewhere. It has stood the test of time, and he might have won the Nobel Prize for this great theory had he not gone on to win it for even more important work.

Two scientific developments in the early 1930s offered that even greater opportunity, which Fermi seized and energetically exploited. The arena for Fermi's new research was experiments with the atomic nucleus. In 1911 British physicist Ernest Rutherford demonstrated the existence of a tiny, positively charged nucleus at the center of all atoms with his experiments on the scattering of alpha particles. (Those alpha particles came from polonium, one of the naturally radioactive elements. We now know that alpha particles consist of two protons and two neutrons bound together—a frequent form of natural radioactivity. But in the 1920s its exact nature was part of the overall mystery of the nucleus.)

Large questions had remained as to the nature of the nucleus. Experiments in Rutherford's laboratory clarified some—but not all—of the issues. What was inside the nucleus? Of what was it made? Some answers came from Rutherford's laboratory where he and his associates demonstrated that alpha particles could not only scatter off atomic nuclei, but could also induce reactions in which the struck nucleus would transform from one nuclear species to another.

Other atom-striking experiments were conducted in Paris by Irène Joliot-Curie (1897–1956) and her husband Frédéric Joliot-Curie (1900–58). They observed penetrating rays that emerged from boron when struck by alpha particles. Unfortunately (it is one of the famous "hard luck" stories of physics) they identified the penetrating rays as gamma rays. They were wrong. In Rutherford's laboratory in 1932, James Chadwick (1891–1974) demonstrated that those penetrating rays were not gamma rays but neutral particles, which he called neutrons.) Prior to Chadwick's discovery, physicists had though that the nuclei of atoms consisted of protons and electrons. They were mistaken. Chadwick showed there were no electrons in the nucleus; rather there was this second, electrically neutral particle along with those positively charged protons. Protons and neutrons—they were the building blocks of all nuclei.

The Joliot-Curies received a Nobel Prize in chemistry for artificially creating radioactivity by bombarding boron and aluminum with alpha particles. Prior to the Joliot-Curies' discovery, radioactivity was a well-known property of the heaviest elements: uranium, thorium, and the like. Indeed Mme. Joliot-Curie's mother, Marie Curie (1867–1934), had been a pioneer in the field of natural radioactive elements, especially radium and polonium. But now there was this new sort of radioactivity—induced or "artificial" radioactivity.

Frédéric Joliot-Curie (left) in the lab with his wife, Irène Joliot-Curie, daughter of Marie Curie. The Joliot-Curies missed discovering the neutron, but went on to win Nobel Prizes of their own.

Fermi seized on these two discoveries—the neutron and artificially induced radioactivity—and merged them. He used neutrons to induce radioactivity. Clearly, it would be easier to penetrate into the target nuclei with the electrically neutral neutrons than with the positively charged alpha particles, which faced the repelling force of the positive charge of the target.

For his neutron source, Fermi used a glass tube containing beryllium powder and radon gas. Alpha particles from the naturally radioactive radon produced neutrons when they struck a beryllium nucleus. Fermi then used

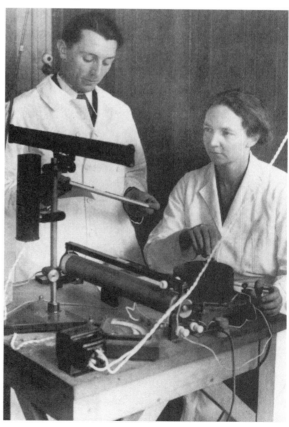

those neutrons to bombard target atoms. Ever the systematic investigator, Fermi started with hydrogen, the very lightest element on the periodic table of the elements. The neutrons did not induce any artificial radioactivity in hydrogen. Similarly negative results followed as he worked his way through the periodic table to heavier elements. Fermi persisted. His first reward came with the element fluorine; irradiated with neutrons, some fluorine nuclei gave off an alpha particle and changed into a radioactive form of nitrogen. Fermi used a Geiger counter to count the electrons, or "beta rays," emitted by the radioactive nitrogen. Aluminum irradiated with neutrons also yielded a radioactive product.

The experimenters measured the induced radioactivity of the nuclei newly created by neutron bombardment. Now, for some elements, the induced radioactivity was weak; for other elements it might decay quickly. In either case, it was important to count the induced activity down the hall, away from the radon source with its relatively high radioactivity. Fermi liked rushing down the corridor to count the short-lived induced radioactivity. In this, as in all things, he enjoyed competition.

Fermi also raced to publish his result in a paper titled "Radioactivity Induced by Neutron Bombardment—I." Fermi boldly added the "I" because he knew he was on a hot trail; he knew there would be many more papers in this series. Working rapidly and systematically, the team— Amaldi, Rasetti, Segrè, and Fermi—irradiated, looked for induced radioactivity, chemically separated the newly created radioactive element, and measured the type of particle emitted, its energy, and how quickly the artificial radiation dwindled. (The latter is called the half-life—the time it takes for the intensity of the induced radioactivity to fall by one half.) Iron, phosphorous, vanadium, uranium, on and on . . . they measured them all.

This was a new sort of high-productivity research, but it was the work of four years of systematic, caring experimentation. The team produced ten papers in the original series and many more besides. Reading those papers today, one can still feel the rush they must have experienced . . . all that data tumbling out, every new element producing its new puzzles. The language of the papers is matter-of-fact, the data presented in orderly scientific columns, but Fermi and his colleagues must have been excited. They were pioneers, explorers—the Lewis and Clark of the nuclear landscape. More than that, they were creating new worlds; the radioactive nuclei produced in that laboratory on Via Panisferna had simply not existed in normal conditions on Earth. All the diversity of nuclear species was laid bare for future study.

Another equally important breakthrough was at hand. In all of their neutron-irradiation studies, the Fermi team had proceeded under the assumption that faster, more energetic neutrons were more effective than slow ones in creating reactions. It is certainly a reasonable assumption—faster, more energy, greater chance of shaking up the target nucleus and making new, radioactive atoms. But Nature had a surprise in store—it is the other way around. Slower neutrons are more effective than their speedier brethren. That became apparent only as the group muddled through some puzzling phenomena.

They began to observe that the amount of induced radioactivity depended on the conditions of irradiation. As Segrè, who worked on this puzzle, tells it: "In particular, there were certain [wooden] tables . . . which had miraculous properties, since silver irradiated on these tables became much more active than when it was irradiated on other, marble tables in the same room." We now know that the effect arises because the wooden table does a better job of slowing neutrons, making them more effective at inducing radioactivity in many elements. But the scientists did not yet know that.

So Segrè and Amaldi set about a systematic investigation of the cause. They used a small lead container to house the irradiation setup. (They were being "systematic" and wanted to standardize the conditions of irradiation.) Fermi had a similar approach in mind, involving the use of a wedge-shaped piece of lead between the neutron source and the target. But, in a wonderful instance of the power of the subconscious mind, Fermi forsook his carefully machined lead wedge in favor of some odd pieces of paraffin—the stuff of candles. That changed everything, for the induced radioactivity was much greater; the Geiger counters clattered away as never before. Induced radioactivity increased by tens or hundreds of times. That slow-neutron discovery, which Fermi called "the most important one I have made," became central to his further work.

What was happening became clear with further experiments. The neutrons were slowed down in collisions with the hydrogen atoms in the paraffin (or in the wood of those tables). The nucleus of the hydrogen atom weighs just about the same as a neutron. So when a neutron collides with a hydrogen atom, the latter takes up a lot of the energy of the neutron—like one billiard ball striking another. But when the neutron hits a heavy nucleus, it is more like the billiard ball hitting a side cushion and bouncing off with no loss of energy. And for many reactions, those slow neutrons were much more effective in inducing radioactivity than fast neutrons were.

In her affectionate biography, *Atoms in the Family,* Laura Fermi tells how the team rushed to see if the effects were repeated with water as the agent slowing the neutrons. They used a goldfish pond in Professor Corbino's garden behind the laboratories.

> On that afternoon of October 22, they rushed their source of neutrons and their silver cylinder [target] to the fountain, and they placed both under water. The goldfish, I am sure, retained their calm and dignity, despite the neutron shower, more than did the crowd outside. The men's excitement was fed on the results of this experiment. It confirmed Fermi's theory. Water also increased the artificial radioactivity of silver by many times.

The discovery of the powerful effects of slow neutrons added similar power to the productivity of the Fermi team. They published at least 25 different papers on neutrons by the end of 1934. By February of 1935, Fermi and his colleagues were able to publish a comprehensive summary of all their work in a British journal, *The Proceedings of the Royal Society (London)*. In it, a lot of the basics of neutron physics is laid out. For example, Fermi shows how slow neutrons pass relatively easily through lead, but are absorbed by very thin layers of the elements cadmium and boron. And Fermi provided the first theory of how neutrons slow down and diffuse in materials such as paraffin. Clearly, there was no one in the world who knew as much about neutrons.

At Corbino's suggestion, Fermi and his colleagues applied for a patent on uses of slow neutrons. It touched on such matters as the production of radioactive atoms and enhancing their production by slowing the neutrons. The patent underlies much of what has been done in the field of nuclear power. In 1953, after much legal wrangling, the government of the United States paid $400,000 for all rights to the patent. Fermi's share, after expenses, was about $24,000, the same as was given to his collaborators.

The stage was set for Fermi to receive physics' highest award: the Nobel Prize. In the fall of 1938, at a scientific conference in Copenhagen, Fermi was approached by the great Danish physicist, Niels Bohr (1885–1962), who asked whether he would be able to accept the Nobel Prize if it were offered to him. That sort of "feeler" had become necessary because fascist governments like those in Germany and Italy had prohibited some prize winners from accepting their awards.

Fermi assured Bohr that he would be open to receiving the prize. Indeed, he had begun to lay plans to leave Italy. Mussolini had started to ape the racial laws of Adolf Hitler's Nazi Germany, laws that restricted the freedom of "non-Aryan" scientists, Jews in particular. Fermi's wife was Jewish, and those racial laws added to Fermi's resolve to leave Italy. His several summer trips to American universities during the preceding decade had made a move to the United States increasingly attractive. He liked Americans and their attitudes. In fact, he had solicited—and quickly received—invitations to teach and do research at American universities. (The Italian authorities were told he was just going for six months.) Now he made plans to go to the United States directly from the Nobel ceremonies in Stockholm.

Those preparations were not in vain because early on the morning of November 10, 1938, the Fermis were told to expect a call that evening from Stockholm. Fermi did not go to work that day, and he and his wife bought watches and other valuables that could get past the Italian authorities in anticipation of their trip. In the evening, waiting for the call from Stockholm, the Fermis listened to the radio, which brought further news of harsh measures against Jews.

Albert Einstein (center left) at a 1933 meeting of the Refugee Assistance Fund in London. Nazi racial laws and persecutions caused many scientists to seek refuge abroad.

Jewish children were excluded from public schools, Jewish teachers were dismissed . . . one cruel (and foolish) law after another. Then the call did come. The secretary of the Swedish Academy of Science read the citation and informed Fermi that the prize was his alone—there was to be no sharing of the prize as in other years. Friends arrived soon thereafter to congratulate Enrico and Laura and to help them forget the bad news on the radio.

King Gustav V of Sweden presented the prize to Fermi on December 10, 1938, the anniversary of Nobel's death. The prize for literature was awarded at the same ceremony—to Pearl Buck, an American novelist. The Nobel Prize ceremony was a grand event, with members of the Swedish Academy, the previous year's winners, and leading lights from the worlds of science, government, and diplomacy present. The principal figures were in formal clothes, so this was one of those very rare occasions when Fermi donned a full-dress formal suit. The Italian government expected him to give a fascist salute, with a stiff, extended arm, on accepting the prize from the king. But Fermi, strongly antifascist, would have none of that, and he simply shook the king's hand. Italian newspapers downplayed the award in retribution. The citation read:

> For his identification of new radioactive elements produced by neutron bombardment and for his discovery, made in conjunction with this work, of nuclear reactions effected by slow neutrons.

The prize was well earned because Fermi had opened the enormous new field of neutron physics. Fermi described his research and credited his collaborators in his acceptance speech, another Nobel Prize tradition.

The final, printed version of that speech contains an interesting footnote in which he acknowledges that the discovery of fission by Otto Hahn and Fritz Strassmann (which was published *after* Fermi received his award and gave his speech) "makes it necessary to re-examine" results

Fermi receives the 1938
Nobel Prize in physics from
King Gustav V of Sweden.

on the transuranic elements." Fermi had erred, believing that the radioactivity he observed when he bombarded uranium with neutrons was due to new elements beyond uranium in the periodic table. He narrowly missed evidence that neutrons could split the uranium atom, that the radioactivity his team observed was from the products of fission, the splitting of uranium.

Not yet aware of fission, Fermi and his family enjoyed a quiet crossing from Southampton to New York on the ocean liner *Franconia*. They arrived on January 2, 1939, and started a new life in a new country.

THE NUCLEAR REACTIONS THAT WON A NOBEL PRIZE

Fermi won the Nobel Prize for the new radioactive elements he created through neutron bombardment. The process he used is one in which an incoming, bombarding neutron penetrates a target nucleus, briefly forms a compound nucleus, which then disgorges a particle of another sort, changing the original nucleus in the process.

To produce neutrons, Fermi employed the same reaction James Chadwick had used in first discovering the neutron. He shot alpha particles at a target of the element beryllium. The alpha particle, the nucleus of the helium atom (chemical symbol He), has two protons and two neutrons, for a total of four nucleons. The shorthand way to write that is: $_2He^4$. The subscript 2 tells us there are two protons; the superscript 4 tells us there are four nucleons total.

Fermi mixed radon, a radioactive source of alpha particles, with beryllium powder. The chemical symbol for beryllium is Be, and the notation for its nucleus is: $_4Be^9$. There are four protons and five (9 minus 4) neutrons.

Now comes the magical part. When a lucky alpha particle penetrates a beryllium nucleus, the following nuclear reaction takes place:

$$_2He^4 + {}_4Be^9 \longrightarrow {}_6C^{12} + 0n^1$$

The beryllium nucleus has been transformed into carbon, and a neutron has been released. Note how the numbers add up and balance on both sides of our equation—subscripts and superscripts both.

Here is the equation describing what happens when one of those neutrons penetrates a fluorine nucleus:

$$_9F^{19} + {}_0n^1 \longrightarrow {}_7N^{16} + {}_2He^4$$

One fluorine nucleus has been transformed into nitrogen, and an alpha particle has been produced. The nitrogen nucleus produced in this reaction is a radioactive *isotope* of nitrogen. The word isotope comes from the Greek words *iso*, meaning same, and *topos*, meaning place. An isotope is a form of an element occupying the *same place* in the periodic table, but having a different number of neutrons. The normal form of nitrogen is $_7N^{14}$ with seven protons and seven neutrons in its nucleus. Figure out how many of each are in $_7N^{16}$.

Albert Einstein
Old Grove Rd.
Nassau Point
Peconic, Long Island

August 2nd, 1939

F.D. Roosevelt,
President of the United States,
White House
Washington, D.C.

Sir:

Some recent work by E.Fermi and L. Szilard, which has been com-
municated to me in manuscript, leads me to expect that the element uranium may be turned into a new and important source of energy in the immediate future. Certain aspects of the situation which has arisen seem
to call for watchfulness and, if necessary, quick action on the part
of the Administration. I believe therefore that it is my duty to bring
to your attention the following facts and recommendations:

In the course of the last four months it has been made probable -
through the work of Joliot in France as well as Fermi and Szilard in
America - that it may become possible to set up a nuclear chain reaction
in a large mass of uranium,by which vast amounts of power and large quant-
ities of new radium-like elements would be generated. Now it appears
almost certain that this could be achieved in the immediate future.

This new phenomenon would also lead to the construction of bombs,
and it is conceivable - though much less certain - that extremely powerful bombs of a new type may thus be constructed. A single bomb of this
type, carried by boat and exploded in a port, might very well destroy
the whole port together with some of the surrounding territory. However,
such bombs might very well prove to be too heavy for transportation by
air.

*The first page of Albert Einstein's 1939 letter to President Franklin D. Roosevelt, warning of uranium chain reac-
tions and bombs. Leo Szilard persuaded Wall Street economist Alexander Sachs, who knew the President, to get
the message through.*

Racing to a Chain Reaction

Word of the discovery of fission spread quickly through the close-knit international physics community. Niels Bohr, the great Danish physicist, brought the news to a seminar at Princeton University. From there it was quickly relayed to Fermi at Columbia University. Fission was something completely new, completely unexpected. Even Fermi had missed it in the careful experiments he had done, experiments that had just won him the Nobel Prize.

Physicists everywhere rushed to study the fission of uranium by slow neutrons. In laboratory after laboratory, they saw the large pulses in their counters and the telltale presence of fission products, elements far below uranium in the periodic table.

The fission reaction was unlike any they had observed before. This was no simple shift from one element to another close by in the periodic table. Fission is a more violent event, one in which a neutron enters a uranium nucleus and causes it to split into two parts. Very importantly, some neutrons are also emitted. One neutron in and more than one neutron out holds the key to possibly creating a chain reaction, one in which those neutrons go on to create still more fissions.

The concept of a nuclear chain reaction had occurred to a remarkable man, the Hungarian-born physicist Leo Szilard (1898–1964), back in 1933. He conjectured that one neutron could create a reaction in which two neutrons were released. He did not know about fission—it had not yet been discovered—but he figured there might be some other reaction that would work. He actually took out a patent, a secret patent that he assigned to the British navy, covering the concept of a nuclear chain reaction and explosives based on it.

By wonderful coincidence, Szilard had gone from Britain to the United States and was working at Columbia University when Fermi arrived just one year later. The two men were quite different. Fermi was very hardworking and systematic, little given to philosophical speculation, still very much the son of a middle-class, middle-level railroad executive. Szilard was a brilliant nonconformist, an "impractical dreamer," who had erratic work habits and was more likely to be found on a park bench— just thinking—seldom troubled by what regulations might demand. Nonetheless, they played complementary roles in going from the basic fact of fission to a chain-reacting device. An even closer co-worker, whose style was like Fermi's, was Herbert Anderson, a young graduate student. Under Fermi's direction, he carried out the first observations of fission at Columbia.

Two considerations added to everyone's eagerness to understand fission. First, there was the enormous energy potential in fission. A mere gram of fully fissioned uranium-235 produces as much energy as 3 tons of coal or 700 gallons of fuel oil. Fission is a million times more potent than ordinary chemical burning, which does not involve changes in the nucleus, only rearrangement of atoms.

Another concern stemmed from international politics. A chain reaction could make a powerful explosive. Fission had first been observed in Germany, and Germany in 1939 was a very aggressive country that had already swallowed up Austria and had designs on Czechoslovakia. Certainly, the many scientists who had fled Germany because of its racial policies did not want a world dominated by Adolf Hitler, the dictator who ruled Germany.

Because of that concern, Szilard urged the physicists to limit the circulation of information about fission, reversing their usual policy of prompt and open publication of scientific results. And later in 1939, Szilard arranged for Albert Einstein to write a letter to President Franklin Delano Roosevelt alerting him to the possibility of powerful new fission weapons. That letter led—slowly—to the creation of an Advisory Committee on Uranium and eventually to the grant of some $6,000 to Columbia to support Fermi's researches. Looking back, it is amazing how sluggish the reaction was to the revolutionary possibility of fission weapons. Even Fermi took off the summers of 1939 and 1940 to lecture at the University of Michigan. But Fermi was a pure scientist, and fission interested him primarily as a phenomenon of nature. He had always avoided politics or any practical application of his research. But as the world's foremost expert on neutron physics, he was reluctantly drawn into the practical work of creating reactors and then bombs. It was not work he would have chosen.

Creating a chain reaction was not going to be easy, even though experiments showed there were about 2.5 neutrons produced per fission. For one thing, the isotope of uranium that was

Hungarian-born physicist Leo Szilard emigrated to Britain and then to the United States. In 1933, he first conceived that a chain reaction could extract energy from the atom, an idea that was scoffed at by others.

fissionable was rare. Uranium has two principal isotopes: uranium-235 and uranium-238. Both have 92 protons in their nuclei, but the heavier isotope has 146 neutrons, three more than in the lighter isotope. Uranium-238 is by far more common; in any natural sample of uranium there are 140 times more uranium-238 atoms than uranium-235. Putting it another way, uranium is only 0.7% uranium-235. Nature had stacked the deck against Fermi.

Another challenge was that the heavier 238 isotope of uranium had a large cross section (that is, a high probability or likelihood) for capturing fast-moving neutrons. That meant those uranium-238 isotopes could gobble up the fast-moving neutrons produced in fission. But Fermi and Szilard thought of a way to beat that problem: have the uranium in small lumps, with material between those lumps that could slow the neutrons—moderate their speed. Lumps of uranium surrounded by moderator, something like that was needed for a chain reaction.

Of course, Fermi knew all about slowing down neutrons; it was a big part of his Nobel Prize research. He knew that paraffin or a similar material could slow the neutrons by collisions with the light elements of which it is made. Slowed neutrons are not as liable to be captured by uranium-238, and slow neutrons would be more efficient at causing further fissions in uranium-235. The supply of neutrons had to be conserved so there would be—on average—at least one neutron surviving from each generation to start the next generation. In his equations, Fermi called that the reproduction factor, k, and the goal of his chain-reaction program was to get k greater than 1.

Fermi considered water as a possible moderator but rejected it because (as he said in a speech years later) "it's very effective in slowing down neutrons, but still absorbs a little bit too many of them, and we could not afford that." He and Szilard decided to try graphite—that black, slippery form of carbon that is in what are mistakenly called "lead" pencils.

Not a lot was known about the absorption properties of graphite, but it was known that it did not absorb a lot. To measure how much graphite did absorb, Fermi did not want to use a small sample and settle for a result with a large uncertainty. Instead, he decided to use what an engineer would call a prototype—a model from which he could learn how the whole approach worked. That would give a more meaningful result, focused on the ultimate goal of a chain reaction with a reproduction factor greater than 1. These experiments, which began in the spring of 1940, were, as Fermi reminisced years later, "the first time that I started to climb on top of my equipment." Physics was becoming a large-scale enterprise.

Fermi and his people piled blocks of graphite to form square columns of graphite, the first of which were three feet on a side and eight feet high. They would place a radon-beryllium neutron source at the base of one of these graphite "piles" (Fermi originated that term) and measure the neutron intensity at varying points along its height. The neutron intensity—measured by the radioactivity induced in rhodium foils—would fall as you went up the column because neutrons were absorbed or scattered out the sides. Fermi could then calculate the properties of graphite from that data. Later they added uranium—in lumps of uranium oxide—systematically spaced throughout those piles.

It was the beginning of a process that would lead to many more such piles and occupy Fermi and his team for the next three years. They overcame great challenges: the purity of graphite had to be improved beyond anything American industry had provided previously. Uranium purity was a similar issue, and chemists at the University of Iowa evolved methods to make it better and better. Szilard was invaluable here; the "impractical dreamer" made it his practical job to find sources of more and purer materials.

The effort grew even more intense after the Japanese bombed Pearl Harbor on December 7, 1941, bringing the

United States into World War II. Germany and Italy joined the Japanese, and that made Fermi an "enemy alien." (It was not until July 1944 that the Fermis became U.S. citizens because the naturalization process requires five years.) Many regulations governed the behavior of enemy aliens. They could not own cameras or shortwave radios. They could not fly in airplanes. If they journeyed outside their own community, they had to "file a statement with the United States District Attorney . . . at least 7 days prior to departure." Enrico Fermi, engaged in this vital war work and commuting often to Chicago, had to secure permission for each trip. Fermi, never one to make a fuss, put up with this bureaucratic rigmarole until it became too burdensome and the bureaucracy found a way to get him a permanent travel pass. Eventually (it was Columbus Day, 1942) the Attorney General ruled that Italians were no longer enemy aliens, and the nettlesome regulations were lifted.

In March 1942, work on chain reactions was consolidated at the University of Chicago at a secret project code-named the Metallurgical Laboratory. Fermi reluctantly moved his team and their piles to Chicago and resumed the battle to get a reproduction factor greater than 1.

Finally, in mid-November 1942, the stage was set for building a pile that could provide a truly self-sustaining chain reaction with the desired reproduction factor. In a rather unlikely place—abandoned squash courts beneath the grandstands of the university's football stadium—Fermi's team gave birth to CP-1, Chicago Pile Number One.

The overall structure was in the form of a slightly squashed sphere, 25 feet wide and 20 feet high. Layer by layer, the team members—aided by husky high-school kids waiting to be drafted—stacked the 400 tons of carefully machined graphite, 40 tons of uranium oxide, and 6 tons of uranium metal. It was hard work, and they worked around the clock—two shifts of 12 hours each.

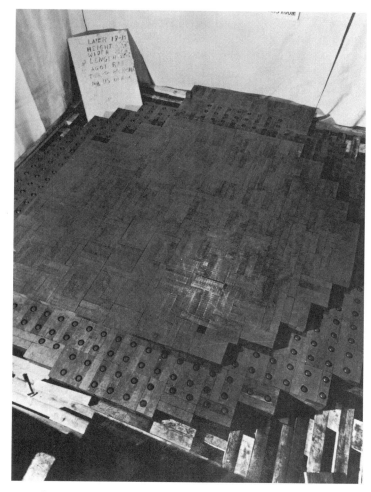

CP-1, the world's first nuclear reactor, under construction. The incomplete top layer is of graphite only; the layer below it contains uranium-oxide "eggs."

Slots in the graphite provided channels for boards covered with neutron-absorbing cadmium—the world's first reactor control rods. ("Reactor" is a term that replaced "pile" in later years.) The tests had shown that this structure could achieve a k greater than 1. It was big enough that the leakage of neutrons out the sides could be tolerated, and it had enough uranium and graphite of sufficient purity to "go critical." Or so Fermi's calculations showed.

The photograph above shows the pile under construction. Layer 19, containing graphite only, is not yet completed, revealing the uranium–oxide "eggs" in the layer below.

There were 22,000 of such uranium lumps, each compacted in a handpress. Al Wattenberg, then a Columbia University graduate student serving on the CP-1 team and now Emeritus Professor of Physics at the University of Illinois, Urbana-Champaign, says, "It was hard work, but exhilarating. We knew we were part of something big, and Fermi was a great leader who saw to it that we all understood how the pile worked. We had total confidence in him."

Still, this was a first—making the first nuclear chain reaction in history—so every reasonable step had to be taken to ensure its success. One unusual step was surrounding the pile with a cubic balloon, somewhat like a huge tent. If necessary, the air could be pumped out, and that would eliminate the neutron absorption from nitrogen in the air. It proved not to be necessary, but it is a nice example of the ingenuity of Fermi and his team.

After each shift, they measured the neutron level in the pile and reported the results to Fermi, who was now too busy with administrative duties to join in the work itself. He calculated how close they were to a self-sustaining chain reaction, to a pile that would give a reproduction factor at least equal to 1. By November 30, with Layer 52 in place, Fermi's careful calculations showed their goal would be reached at Layer 56. Ever-conservative, he called for an extra layer—number 57—to be put in place by the night shift on December 1. He made Herbert Anderson promise to resist the temptation to withdraw the control rods and make the chain reaction self-sustaining. The layers were added, and the control rods were locked in place, as he had directed.

Fermi assembled the team the morning of Wednesday, December 2, 1942. He was fully confident of his understanding of how his pile would behave, but to protect against any unforeseen effects, there were safety measures. A control rod would automatically fall into place and shut down the pile if the neutron intensity (measured by electronic counters) got too high. As a backup to that, there was another safety rod supported by a rope that could be cut with an ax, causing the rod to drop into the pile. Finally there was a "suicide squad," three young physicists equipped with jugs of neutron-absorbing cadmium sulfate to pour into the pile if something went haywire.

With safety attended to, Fermi went to work. He wanted to proceed systematically to bring the pile to a self-sustaining condition. First he confirmed that the neutron intensity with the control rods fully in was the same as Anderson had measured it the evening before. Then he directed George Weil, the young physicist responsibile for adjusting the one remaining cadmium control rod, to pull it out halfway. As expected, the neutron intensity increased, then leveled off. Fermi could tell things were going as planned from the sound of the counters, but he was not content until he measured the neutron level and calculated its rate of growth. He then calculated how close they were to self-sustaining, using his slide rule, that clever device that can multiply, divide, and calculate logarithms by moving a ruler-like middle piece within two fixed ones. In Fermi's hands, it could do all the calculations he needed.

Satisfied with those numbers, Fermi called on Weil to pull the rod out another six inches. Then he carefully checked the rate of increase and the intensity at which it leveled off. More slide-rule calculation, and Fermi called on Weil to pull the rod out another six inches. Everything was on track. Another withdrawal and its set of measurements followed. And then another.

Each time the counters grew faster, in keeping with the growing neutron intensity—and then leveled off at their new and higher tempo. By now the rates were so high that some of the instruments had to be adjusted to cover the new range. Fermi checked that the readings at the new ranges agreed with the earlier ones. Then he instructed Weil to pull the rod out another six inches. Up went the intensity; then CRASH!—the automatic safety rod slammed into its slot—as it was designed to do.

Cool as always, confident that all was going well, Fermi called for everyone to break for lunch. ("I'm hungry! Let's go to lunch," he is reported to have said.) Another researcher might have pressed on, eager to go critical and attain a self-sustaining chain reaction as soon as possible. Not Fermi. For one thing, he was always deliberate in both thought and action. For another thing, he is Italian, and lunch on time is a ritual in Italy, one that survived his emigration to the United States and the urgencies of wartime research. The control rods were reinserted and locked in place, and everyone went off to eat.

Whatever may have been on the menu that day, it was surely accompanied by a great sense of controlled excitement. Everyone wanted to be cool like Fermi—at least on the surface. But this was the payoff for months of work, tons of uranium pressed into "eggs," and endless logs of sooty graphite machined and lugged into place. Back to work they went. The safety rod was withdrawn, and the neutron intensity at which it would drop was raised. Weil brought his control rod, by stages, back to the position it was in before lunch. The neutron intensity was now high enough that Fermi could follow the trace of the pen that displayed the intensity automatically on a chart. That would not have been feasible at lower intensities. Fermi extracted meaning from that chart with further manipulation of his slide rule. He was now just one step away from the self-sustaining level; Weil need only pull his control rod out another foot.

But Fermi did something that might have surprised a layman. He had the safety rod reinserted, this time deliberately. He wanted to bring the intensity down to a low value, so that he could follow its rise over an even greater range. Next he had Weil pull the one remaining rod farther than ever before—another 12 inches. Only then was the safety rod withdrawn. This time there was no leveling off.

The intensity grew and grew; Fermi's eyes fixed first on the chart recorder then on the slide rule, darting back and forth. Still no leveling off.

Observers remember Fermi's words: "The reaction is self-sustaining." And they remember his broad, broad smile.

Fermi allowed the intensity to grow for yet another 11 minutes, then called for all rods to be reinserted and locked. The maximum power reached was only half a watt, but from that puny beginning a potent new source of energy and destruction was mankind's to use—or misuse.

It was a time for celebration, and Hungarian-born physicist Eugene Wigner (1902–95), who rivaled Fermi in his understanding of pile theory, was equal to the occasion. He had brought a bottle of Italian Chianti. Paper cups were secured from a water cooler, and all hands saluted what they had accomplished. With a fine sense of history, most of them signed the straw wrapper that is a hallmark of a bottle of Chianti.

There was no hilarity. Those who were present and have written about the occasion seem to emphasize the silence, even the solemnity. Wigner himself has written, in his memoir *Symmetries and Reflections*, "For some time we had known that we were about to unlock a giant; still, we could not escape an eerie feeling when we knew we had actually done it [with] far-reaching consequences [we could not] foresee."

Arthur Compton, as head of the Metallurgical Laboratory, was pleased to report by telephone in a coded message to James Conant, the government's top civilian research chief, that "The Italian navigator has just landed in the new world."

It was a new world. Leo Szilard, who first conceived of a chain reaction, stayed on after the crowd had left, shook hands with Fermi, and said that he thought "this day would go down as a black day in the history of mankind." There was cause for such

Most of the CP-1 team signed the basket of this bottle of Chianti bought by Eugene Wigner to celebrate the pile going critical on December 2, 1942.

worry. Terrible new weapons were now closer to reality. By now powerful piles that would produce plutonium for use in atomic bombs were being designed. Fermi was to play a major role in that phase too.

In the weeks that followed, Fermi and his team continued their effort to obtain pile materials of even greater purity. They also found the pile to be a wonderful tool for studying the behavior of neutrons because it could provide a steady source more intense than any they had used before. That helped them in their next major chore, the design and construction of a new, more powerful pile at a more isolated location outside of Chicago. This pile, CP-2, operated at a power level of 100,000 watts—far beyond the 0.5 watt at which Fermi had run CP-1 that first, historic day. By November 1943, there was yet another uranium-graphite pile, the air-cooled X-10, at yet another laboratory, this one in Oak Ridge, Tennessee.

Before going on with the story of Enrico Fermi's contributions to the development of nuclear weapons, here are two important points left out of our discussion of piles. The first is: "Why are piles so easy to control? Why don't they blow up . . . as atomic bombs do?" It is a good question, and the answer lies in the fact that a certain proportion of the neutrons emitted in fission are delayed. Specifically, three quarters of a percent of the neutrons come out in a time that ranges from 1.5 to as many as 55.6 seconds. These delayed neutrons do not come directly from the fissioning uranium nucleus; rather, they come from further decay processes in some of the fission products. So the last three quarters of a percent—0.0075—of a pile's chain reaction comes from delayed neutrons, and that helps in the control of a pile.

Of course, if too much uranium fuel is loaded into a pile and its control rods are yanked out too far, it can get critical without the delayed neutrons, and reactor accidents have occurred that way.

The second and vital point is that the capture of a neutron by the heavy isotope, uranium-238 leads to the formation of the isotope uranium-239. It then undergoes radioactive decay, transforming into the element neptunium, followed by further decay to plutonium-239, which is fissionable. Thus piles could produce not only energy but also another fissionable element.

In World War II, the United States pursued two paths to an atomic bomb. The first was to produce plutonium in nuclear piles. The second approach was to separate the fissionable uranium-235 isotopes from the much more abundant (but not fissionable) uranium-238 isotopes. With wartime urgency, the United States followed both approaches, and both succeeded—a most remarkable accomplishment.

Enormously important to that accomplishment was a military man, Major General Leslie R. Groves (1896–1970). In mid-September 1942 Groves, then a colonel, was put in charge of the entire atom-bomb project, code-named the Manhattan Engineering District. Groves was accustomed to big projects and bold decisions; he had been deputy chief of all construction for the U.S. army and supervised the construction of the Pentagon. He knew how to give orders and get things done fast. Under its civilian leadership, the project had started slowly and had been subject to one review after another. Groves was prepared to take big risks, make mistakes, and try multiple approaches in order to move ahead.

General Groves had an abiding concern for security. When he took over direction of the atomic bomb project, he instituted new measures to further ensure secrecy and the safety of top scientists.

Those top scientists were given code names, to be used when traveling or otherwise dealing with the outside world. Dr. Enrico Fermi became Mr. Eugene Farmer; Niels Bohr became Nicholas Baker; Wigner became Wagner, and so forth. (Not very deceptive names, it would seem, but the thinking of security personnel is sometimes mysterious.) In Fermi's *Collected Papers*, one piece bears the name E. Farmer as author. And when Mrs. Fermi first came to Los Alamos, the soldier who met her at the railroad station asked, "Are you Mrs. Farmer?" She replied, "Yes, I'm Mrs. Fermi," whereupon the soldier said, mildly but with reproving eyes, "I was told to call you Mrs. Farmer."

Fermi was also given a full-time personal bodyguard early in 1943. The guard—a member of Army military intelligence in plain clothes—was a six-foot, 200-pound, cheerful, recent law-school graduate named John Baudino. He was Fermi's constant companion, joining him on all car trips to Argonne and on train trips to Hanford and elsewhere. Baudino and Fermi came to be good friends, playing gin rummy on those train trips, and Baudino occasionally lent a hand in the laboratory when that was appropriate. When Fermi and his family moved to Los Alamos, Baudino and his wife and infant daughter moved there too. He stayed at Fermi's side until the war was over.

In a directive from Groves, Fermi was instructed to "refrain from flying in airplanes of any description; the time saved is not worth the risk . . . refrain from driving an automobile for any appreciable distance . . . and from being without suitable protection on any lonely road."

Groves also convinced the Du Pont Corporation, the giant U.S. chemical corporation, to assume responsibility for the construction of giant piles in Hanford, Washington. This was to be an enormous scale-up; Fermi's CP-1 had never operated at a power of more than 200 watts; the three Hanford production piles were each to operate at 250 million watts. The issues were now as much chemistry and engineering as physics: How would they cool these multimegawatt piles? How could the chemists process the dangerously radioactive fission products and extract the fissionable plutonium for further purification and processing into bomb material?

Not surprisingly, there was a clash of cultures—engineers and physicists have different approaches. Engineers are more practical, prepared to approximate and compensate for

The huge plutonium-pro-
duction complex on the
Columbia River in Hanford,
Washington. Each
water-cooled reactor had
2,004 channels holding
aluminum-clad uranium
slugs.

those approximations with safety factors; physicists are more
given to an approach based on theory alone. But both
groups recognized the urgency of what they were doing.
The war was raging fiercely, and this project could help win
it. Despite that urgency and the efforts of some 42,000 construction workers, it was September 1944 before the first of
the Hanford piles went critical. But they did the job; plutonium for the first atomic bomb was delivered in time for
the first test of such a weapon. It was a test in which Fermi
would play an interesting role.

Fermi (third from left) and teammates at Los Alamos in late 1943. Others include (left to right): Herbert Anderson, D. Froman, H. Barschall, R. R. Wilson, Joe Fowler, John Manley, Seth Neddermeyer, L.D.P. King, Egon Bretscher, Emilio Segrè, and Hans Staub.

Los Alamos and the A-Bomb

It was called the Los Alamos Ranch School. It had been founded in 1917 as a place to which rich parents could send their sickly sons to build them up physically as well as to learn. It was beautifully situated in the Sangre de Christo mountains on a 7,200-foot mesa above the valley of the Rio Grande, some 35 miles northwest of Sante Fe, New Mexico. But now it was to be disbanded; the U.S. Army would take over the school and the surrounding land for a project so secret it bore only the name Site Y. Here would rise the laboratory that would develop the atom bomb.

In June 1942 General Groves chose J. Robert Oppenheimer (1904–67), a brilliant theoretical physicist, to head the A-bomb effort. (Oppenheimer had led intense theoretical studies at the University of California on how to make a bomb.) Together they selected Los Alamos as the site for the new weapons laboratory. Los Alamos was a marvelous place for a secret laboratory. It was isolated, with just one steep, winding dirt road. That would help ensure security, even though it proved daunting to newcomers to The Hill. Scientists could conduct dangerous experiments with explosives in the deep ravines. The trails for hiking and skiing, streams for fishing, and much natural beauty were sure to refresh the spirits of the scientific teams that would soon assemble there.

Oppenheimer staffed Los Alamos with the very cream of American nuclear physics and chemistry. It became the center for what was to swell to more than 2,500 people. They lived a pioneer life at first, scattered among nearby dude ranches and putting up with all sorts of shortages and inconveniences. Jane Wilson, wife of physicist Robert Wilson, recalls that streets were unpaved, with mud everywhere; soot from the soft coal used to heat the houses covered everything. The school's stone and log building served as headquarters, and the homes formerly occupied by the headmaster and teachers were available only to the top laboratory personnel. Those houses had bathtubs, giving the name "Bathtub Row" to that part of town. Elsewhere it was a boomtown filled with a chaotic array of trailers and

This house on "Bathtub Row," originally the Los Alamos Ranch School arts and crafts building, was used as the home for the laboratory director. The Jemez mountain range is in the background.

houses hastily constructed of green lumber or prefabricated sections. They had modern refrigerators, but the huge wood- and coal-burning cooking stoves were so difficult to use that many residents settled for electric hot plates even though they were vulnerable to power outages.

The people of Los Alamos had to get used to living in a community surrounded by fences and barbed wire. Mail was censored, long-distance calls were monitored, and badges were required for entrance. All incoming mail was addressed to Box 1663 in Santa Fe; Los Alamos did not exist as a post office address. But almost everyone was young and willing to put up with inconveniences—Project Y was extremely important and could help win the war.

By April 1943 the top scientists assembled to organize their program of research. "Oppie," as Oppenheimer was called, led the intense discussions. Fermi was there for this first planning meeting, and he later came full-time to serve as associate director and to head one of its divisions.

The goal at Los Alamos was to produce a weapon, a bomb so powerful it would help the United States and its allies win the terrible world war then raging. Because fission releases so much more energy than even the most explosive chemical reactions, an atomic bomb would be more powerful than any bomb in history. Fission was millions of times more powerful than chemical energy. Just one kilogram—2.2 pounds—of plutonium-239 or uranium-235, completely fissioned, had the explosive power of about 20,000 tons of TNT.

In an atomic bomb, there would be no moderator—no neutron-slowing graphite as was needed in Fermi's piles. Slow neutrons were just too slow for the job. Here the idea was to use fast neutrons, just as they came out of the fissioning nucleus. Without a moderator, the chain reaction would build up explosively—fast beyond all ordinary experience, but not beyond the ability of those Los Alamos scientists to comprehend, calculate, and eventually measure.

Less than a millionth of a second is all it would take. And the release of all that energy in so short a time would lead to temperatures unknown on Earth—about 10 billion degrees.

Here is a rough picture of how that explosion builds: An initial fission in a sphere of uranium-235 or plutonium-239 produces two fast neutrons (actually there were more than two, but for simplicity, say two). Within a billionth of a second, those two strike two other nuclei and produce 4, then 8, then 16, 32, more, more, 1,024, 2,048, each new generation coming superfast on the heels of the preceding. This is all done with neutrons moving quickly, swiftly striking yet another nucleus. It takes only about 80 generations to fission all the nuclei in a kilogram, a millionth of a second all told. And each fission releases atomic energy. Temperatures reach billions of degrees as all that energy is released in that small space.

Making such a bomb was a huge job, unlike any ever faced before. Those scientists assembling in Los Alamos had a theory of how an A-bomb would work, but now they needed facts and numbers. Just how many fast neutrons came out when plutonium-239 (or uranium-235) fissioned, and how fast did they emerge, and how fast were they moving? The researchers had to learn all they could about uranium and plutonium. They would need new superhigh-speed cameras and X-ray machines to follow the workings of an A-bomb. All that and much more was needed to make a "gadget." ("Gadget" was the code word used in place of "atomic bomb.")

After Fermi attended that initial meeting, he became an important, if occasional, consultant to Los Alamos. He came even though he continued to have big jobs elsewhere, such as advising on the huge plutonium production reactors under construction in Hanford, Washington. That was a huge undertaking in itself, and it was nearly undone by a problem that had not been fully anticipated—the "poisoning" of the first pile by certain products of fission.

Fermi would have come to Los Alamos earlier, but he was delayed by an unexpected problem at the Hanford plutonium production piles. Fermi and Leona Marshall, part of his team at CP-1, were there for the startup, checking the readings as the pile went critical—first at low power without cooling water and then with the full force of cooling water from the Columbia River flowing through it. All seemed well; here was a pile at 250 megawatts, far above the power level of its predecessors in Chicago. But then a strange thing began to happen. The reactor operators had to withdraw the control rods further and further to keep the power level where it was supposed to be. Finally the control rods had to be withdrawn their full length, and yet the power level continued to fall lower. By the evening of the next day, the chain reaction had stopped, and the reactor died completely.

Then an even stranger thing: the reactor came back to life, ran for several hours, and then lost power again. What was wrong? Fermi could see that the pile was being "poisoned." There was a product of fission and perhaps a further danger from the decay of that fission product that had an enormous ability to absorb neutrons. The culprits turned out to be radioactive forms of the elements iodine and xenon. The radioactive iodine (iodine-135) was formed as one of the fission products of uranium-235. It then decayed, with half of it decaying in 6.7 hours, into xenon-135. That form of xenon had a perfectly enormous appetite for neutrons—absorption far beyond anything known before. And that would soak up neutrons and kill the reactivity of the pile. But the xenon itself would decay and disappear, with a half-life of 9.13 hours. With that poison gone, the pile could go critical again.

Fortunately, Eugene Wigner, who had worked with the Du Pont engineers in the design of the Hanford piles, had anticipated the possibility of such pile poisons. They had included space for additional uranium, to add enough fissions to overcome potential problems and keep the reactor going. It required some new cooling channels for the added uranium, but in time Hanford Pile B could be taken critical again and stay in operation. It was a close call with a happy ending.

Resolving that problem allowed Fermi to turn his full attention to Los Alamos in September of 1944, a year and a half after Site Y was founded. (Mrs. Fermi and the children came on their own because Fermi was occupied with the startup at Hanford. She found lots of old friends there: the Tellers, the Bethes, the Rossis, and Emilio Segrè, among others. She had been alerted in advance, so she and the children brought boots, to deal with the ever-present mud, as well as a large dose of patience for the inevitable hassles of living under army rules. But they also found young people, lots of parties, and a social life that made it easier to live with censored mail and no telephone.)

Fermi knew Los Alamos was the payoff, the final step in the long path to an atomic bomb. Oppenheimer was eager to have his help and made Fermi an associate director and the leader of a special division, Division F. It was also known as the Problem Division because it handled special situations and difficult people. Chief among the latter was Edward Teller, a brilliant theoretician who did not want to work on fission but only on the "Super"—code name for early efforts to create the even more powerful hydrogen bomb. Fermi also became boss of a physicist named L.D.P. King, whose group worked on a small, very low-power reactor that had been built at Los Alamos to serve as a neutron source for research purposes. Nicknamed "the water boiler," it was a simple one-foot-diameter spherical vessel containing a solution of uranium salt in water. It was the world's first reactor using enriched uranium—uranium with more than the 0.7% uranium-235 of natural uranium. (The enriched uranium came from the huge separation plants that had been constructed in Oak Ridge, Tennessee, in the second approach to an atom bomb.)

Another component of the Fermi Division was formed in November 1944 when his longtime collaborator, Herbert Anderson, came down from Chicago's Metallurgical Laboratory to join him. He and his people made vital contributions, developing a method to determine the efficiency of the first atomic bomb.

A crucial question concerned the "critical mass"—the amount of fissionable material needed to make a bomb. (With too small an amount, the bomb would fizzle as neutrons escaped out the side. With too large an amount, precious nuclear material would be wasted as the bomb exploded.) To learn more about fast neutrons, Los Alamos researchers needed nuclear accelerators. Such "machines" could push protons (or other suitable nuclei) to energies high enough to produce high-energy neutrons when they struck suitable targets. There was no time to build new ones, so the physicists at Los Alamos did something typical of the bold moves throughout the Manhattan Project: nuclear accelerators were trucked in from universities around the country. Harvard University contributed its *cyclotron*—the sort of accelerator that sends protons or other light nuclei around in an ever-increasing circular path in a fixed magnetic field, giving them another push in each cycle till high energies are reached. (The "push" came from an alternating electric field timed to match the frequency at which the particles move in their circular paths.)

The University of Wisconsin team brought two Van de Graaff accelerators—machines that bring protons to high energy with a powerful electric field that is itself generated by transporting electric charges on a fast-moving belt. Unlike the cyclotron, this is a steady electric field. Yet another machine came from the University of Illinois.

It was an exciting time. The American physics community rallied to meet the challenge of building an atomic bomb. Would they succeed in that awesome task? And were the Germans ahead of them? After all, Germany was the country where fission had been discovered. And Germany was a leader in science—Oppenheimer himself had gone to Göttingen in Germany to get his doctoral degree. Led by Adolf Hitler, the Germans could have gone from fission experiments to a fission bomb. There was no way to know—the Germans were as good at keeping secrets as the Americans . . . maybe better, with their closed, dictatorial society. Everyone at Los Alamos felt that pressure.

Even before bringing their accelerators to Los Alamos, the Wisconsin researchers, Joe McKibben and graduate student David Frisch, had run those machines around the clock for many months to get crucial data on the behavior of fast neutrons. They did for fast neutrons what Fermi had done for slow neutrons back in Rome—a careful survey of how fast neutrons behaved in various materials. They knew that such data would be needed for the design of an atomic bomb, and they were determined to get it.

The Wisconsin team got the larger of their two accelerators into operation at Los Alamos on May 15, 1943. They went on to do an even more vital measurement: the fission of plutonium by fast neutrons. Their plutonium sample was

Saturday night concerts at the Fuller Lodge were welcomed by a Los Alamos staff members who worked long hours six—and sometimes seven—days a week.

very tiny, barely visible, just 142 millionths of a gram. But that speck was enough for their measurements.

Team members worked 18 to 20 hours a day during this period, but they got the crucial measurements done. The experiments confirmed that plutonium would fission and produce enough neutrons quickly enough. Indeed, plutonium-239 produced more neutrons per fission than did uranium-235. (Their tiny sample of plutonium was produced in a cyclotron at Washington University in St. Louis; the Hanford plants were still more than a year away from operation. Those huge plants were being built at Hanford on the *assumption* that plutonium-239 would work in a bomb.)

Things looked good for a plutonium bomb, but one more huge hurdle remained. That problem had been anticipated on theoretical grounds by Fermi, and the critical measurements that revealed it were performed by Emilio Segrè, his former student and collaborator, who had also migrated to America and come to Los Alamos via the University of California at Berkeley. The problem lay in the high spontaneous fission rate of plutonium-240. To understand why that was a problem, it is necessary to take a closer look at how an atomic bomb works.

Los Alamos pursued two paths to an atomic bomb. They differed in the fissionable material used. One used uranium-235, the light isotope of uranium. It was being painstakingly separated from the more common uranium-238 in giant factories in Oak Ridge, Tennessee. The other approach used plutonium-239, that was soon to be produced from those giant piles still under construction at at Hanford, Washington.

The basic idea of an atomic bomb is simple: assemble pieces of fissionable material so rapidly and with so much force that a chain reaction can go through enough generations before the "gadget" blows itself apart from the energy released in all those fissions. One way to do this is by shooting a heavy "bullet" of uranium-235 into a target of uranium-235. This "gun" approach is needed because bullet and target need to be brought together very quickly lest the chain reaction start prematurely and the bomb blow itself apart and thus fizzle.

Of course, an actual bomb is much more complex: a "tamper" is needed to hold the parts in place and bounce neutrons back just that extra fraction of a millionth of a second longer while the nuclear chain reaction builds. You also need an "initiator" to start the chain reaction just when you want the bomb to go off. This gun arrangement does work for uranium-235 and was the basis for the bomb used in Hiroshima.

The gun approach does not work for plutonium. In fact, a major crisis developed with the plutonium approach. That crisis threatened to make all of Fermi's work and the giant plants being built at Hanford useless; it was the major crisis of the wartime atom-bomb effort and almost led Oppenheimer to resign.

The problem is that plutonium-239 produced in a pile is accompanied by a certain amount of plutonium-240. Those plutonium-240 isotopes were inevitably formed as some of the 239 version captured yet another neutron in the blizzard of neutrons inside a pile. And that slightly heavier isotope could fission spontaneously, without being part of a chain reaction.

Was that not good? Was it not fission that you wanted? Well, yes, but not too many fissions occurring spontaneously. That could set off the chain reaction before the pieces of the bomb came fully together. It would not explode; it would predetonate weakly and fizzle. There was so much spontaneous fission in pile plutonium that even the fastest guns brought the pieces together too slowly. The gun approach would not work for plutonium. A tragedy, it seemed.

Fortunately, a Los Alamos scientist named Seth Neddermeyer had been pursuing another way to bring the pieces of a bomb together. Instead of a gun arrangement, Neddermeyer chose an approach that others felt was too difficult. In his approach, the bomb material is brought to a supercritical state superfast by imploding it. (*Im*ploding is the opposite of *ex*ploding. The prefix *ex* means out, and *im* means in.) Imagine squeezing a ball of clay with both your hands. Now imagine a squeezing force that comes equally from all directions. That force can create an implosion.

With implosion, a critical mass could be created and the bomb set off even faster than with a gun, even before spontaneous fission could cause it to pre-trigger. Implosion, the opposite of explosion, would lead to the greatest explosions in all history.

Overcoming the technical problems associated with the implosion approach required a big buildup in the staff of Los Alamos. And it required Neddermeyer to hand leadership of the implosion effort over to Professor George Kistiakowsky, who came from Harvard University to add his unmatched knowledge of high explosives to the Los Alamos effort. In the end, however, high explosives became something they could control at will. They created high-explosive "lenses" much like optical lenses, and could create shock waves that could squeeze from every direction toward the center and create an implosion. To enable the researchers to see what they had accomplished, other Los Alamos teams developed wonderful high-speed X-ray machines that showed the implosion as it progressed.

It worked. It was not easy, but the talented men and women of Los Alamos solved the very tough problem of creating a spherical implosion. They learned, in experiment after experiment, how to get a carefully designed group of high explosives to go off in just the right submicrosecond sequence. The resulting implosion could compress a sphere to densities twice normal, and do it faster than a chain reaction could blow it apart. A supercompressed sphere of plutonium would be supercritical—a bomb.

That sort of technical daring and hard work brought solutions to the many other problems involved in building an atomic bomb. In February 1945, even though problems remained, General Groves ordered a design freeze. There were to be no more changes to the A-bomb plans. That way everything could be ready for a test in July. By July they expected to have enough plutonium produced at Hanford to be able to complete a first bomb.

The test was so complicated that planning for it had begun more than a year before. In February 1945, when test preparations grew really intense, 250 people worked on them. The test was conducted 210 miles south of Los Alamos, in an 18-by-25-mile section of an army air force bombing range. Oppenheimer gave the site and the test itself the code name "Trinity."

Smart experimenters that they were, the test team first tested the test in order to check out their instruments and plans. To do this, in May 1945, they exploded 100 tons of high explosives at the Trinity site. They had added radioactive fission products from the Hanford plant to check the mea-

Norris Bradbery (left) with the completely assembled Trinity plutonium bomb, in its tower on July 15, 1945. The test bomb was successfully detonated the next day.

surements they would be doing on the radioactivity from the atomic bomb. It was the largest such man–made chemical explosion ever, but it would soon be dwarfed by the A–bomb test itself. Fermi played a special role during the test preparations. He was said to be the one person whose knowledge of both theory and experiment was equal to the many different aspects of this test that involved so many branches of physics.

Finally the time came to test the world's first atomic bomb. The bomb, a plutonium implosion type, was carefully assembled at the Trinity site and raised to the top of a

Test of the Trinity bomb on July 16, 1945. The blast from this explosion was the equivalent of about 20,000 tons of TNT; sand at the base of the tower melted to glass.

100-foot tower. It consisted of several main parts: at its center was an initiator—a bit of polonium and beryllium, the classic ingredients for a neutron source. The initiator would provide the first few neutrons to get the tremendous chain reaction going. Around it was a solid ball of plutonium-239, not yet sufficiently dense to be of critical size. Surrounding that was a tamper of natural uranium . . . not capable of fission, but heavy enough to carry out two critical functions. The first was to bounce neutrons back into the chain reaction once it got underway, and the second function was to hold the bomb together in those billionths of a second as it built to full fury. Surrounding that tamper was some 5,000 pounds of high explosive of two sorts, carefully designed and produced to create the spherical shock wave to implode the tamper and compress the plutonium, making it supercritical. The initiator was also crushed together, producing the first few neutrons that got the chain reaction going.

The automated countdown began at T (the time set for the explosion) minus 45 seconds. Only one man, physicist Donald Hornig, had a switch that could stop it after that. "I don't think I have ever been keyed up as I was during those final seconds," he told an interviewer years later.

The countdown proceeded. Everyone was tense. All the work of the past six years hung on the result. General Groves wrote, in his autobiography, *Now It Can Be Told*: "As we approached the final minute, the quiet grew more intense. . . . I thought only what I would do if the countdown got to zero and nothing happened."

But something did happen. The bomb was set off on Monday, July 16, 1945, at 5:29 in the morning. The blast from this modest amount—about ten pounds—of plutonium was the equivalent of about 20,000 tons of TNT. The tower from which the "gadget" had been suspended was completely vaporized. Sand at the base of the tower was melted to glass. A 300-foot crater was carved in the desert floor. There had been nothing like it in the history of humankind.

Here, in his own words, is Fermi's description of that awesome event, taken from a report once marked "Secret": "Although I did not look directly toward the object, I had the impression that suddenly the countryside became brighter than in full daylight. I subsequently looked in the direction of the explosion through the dark [welder's] glass and could see something like a conglomeration of flames that promptly started rising. After a few seconds, the rising flames lost their brightness and appeared as a huge pillar of smoke with an expanding head like a gigantic mushroom that rose rapidly beyond the clouds . . . to a height of 30,000 feet."

Another observer, the physicist I. I. Rabi (1898–1988), spoke of "an enormous flash of light, the brightest light I have ever seen. It blasted; it pounced; it bored its way right through you. It was a vision that was seen with more than the eye. . . . It looked menacing. It seemed to come toward one."

Emilio Segrè wrote of "overwhelmingly bright light. . . . I thought the explosion might set fire to the atmosphere and thus finish the earth, even though I knew that was not possible."

Oppenheimer, director of this now successful project, remembered some lines from the Hindu scripture, the *Bhagavad-Gita*: "Now I am become Death, the destroyer of worlds."

There was deep truth in those words. Not many days later—on August 6, 1945—a single B-29 bomber, the Enola Gay, with Colonel Paul Tibbets in charge, dropped a uranium gun-type bomb on Hiroshima, Japan. Some 200,000 people died as a result of that one bomb.

On August 9 the U.S. dropped a second bomb, this time the implosion, plutonium sort, on Nagasaki. Its force was estimated at 22,000 tons of TNT. Some 70,000 people died by year-end and that many more over the next five years.

Faced with this terrible toll, Hirohito, the Japanese Emperor, called on his military leaders to surrender.

This implosion-type plutonium bomb, called Fat Man, was dropped on Nagasaki on August 9, 1945. President Harry S. Truman gave the order to drop the bomb after warning the Japanese that they would be destroyed if they did not surrender.

Without question, the atomic bomb shortened the war because the Japanese were prepared to fight on and on, despite the conventional bombing they had previously endured.

Debate over whether these two atomic bombs should have been dropped continues to this day. On the one hand, there was a war on, and nonnuclear weapons such as the firebombing of Tokyo had also killed 100,000 in a single night raid. Also, thousands of American soldiers, sailors, and marines faced likely death in the planned invasion of Japan. The Japanese had vowed to fight on and would surely have fought hard to protect their homeland. An American soldier could only feel good that the war was shortened and he was still alive.

On the other hand, scientists such as Leo Szilard had argued for a demonstration explosion, to be witnessed by Japanese scientists and others. The idea was to convince them of the power of these new weapons without killing so many in the process. Such voices went unheeded; it would prove hard for them to get a hearing in the rush to complete, test, and use the bomb. It is still a fit subject for debate, though it is difficult today to recapture the intense feelings—of hatred and of fear—during a war.

Other voices called for a better recognition that the nature of war had been changed by these weapons of ultimate power. Fermi had a role, as a member of a scientific panel to advise the government on postwar policy. The panel warned that atomic weapons might make a nation strong, but that the true safety of the nation rested on "making future wars impossible."

That noble goal has been reached only in part. There has been no further use of atomic weapons in war. But there have been wars—lots of them, with lots of deaths in lots of countries—in the decades since Hiroshima and Nagasaki. In this, as in so many areas, our ability to advance technology is not yet matched by our ability to resolve conflicts.

An atomic bomb explodes over Nagasaki and ends World War II.

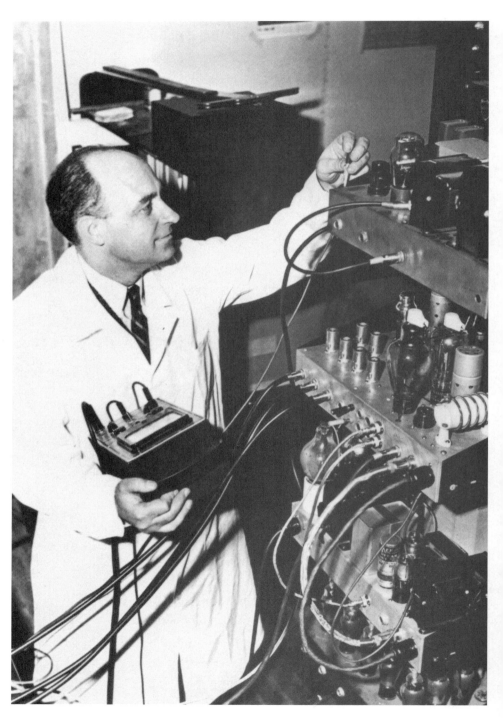

Fermi tests the electronic controls for a neutron time-of-flight, velocity-selector device. Wartime advances in electronics made it easier to measure cross sections as a function of neutron energy.

Science in Chicago, Service in Washington

With the war over and the great successes at CP-1, Hanford, and Los Alamos behind him, Fermi faced some major decisions. So did the nation as a whole.

The United States, with its allies, had won World War II. The United States alone had this very powerful new weapon—the atomic bomb. That brought great military power, but it also gave America a grave responsibility: how much should it share of its knowledge of atomic energy? The scientists and engineers who had created the bomb knew that atomic energy was more than just the atomic bomb. There was important new science, the science of the nucleus. And there were applications of atomic energy in nonmilitary areas, such as generating electricity or curing disease. A fight was brewing between the military and the scientists. Fermi was drawn into the fight over control of atomic energy, even though he always believed that scientists had no special qualification in political matters.

It was a great time to be a physicist. The wartime accomplishments in radar and atomic weapons had emphasized how important science was to the power of a nation—in peace and in war. Arthur Roberts, a multitalented physicist at the University of Rochester, celebrated the newly recognized importance of physicists in an album of songs, one of which ran,

> How nice to be a physicist in 1947. . .
> How nice to be a physicist in this our year of grace,
> To see the scornful world at last admit your rightful place,
> To see the senators defer to every wise pronouncement,
> To fascinate the women's club, and star at each
> commencement . . .

If it was a great time for all physicists, it was an especially good time for a Nobel Prize winner such as Enrico Fermi. He could have had his pick of professorships at universities throughout the world.

Fermi chose to return to the University of Chicago. Exciting things were happening there under its young president, Robert Maynard Hutchins. Even though he was not a scientist, Hutchins saw the new postwar importance of the sciences. He supported a plan, proposed by Arthur Compton, the wartime head of the Metallurgical Laboratory at Chicago, to create three new institutes in the sciences. Foremost among them was the Institute for Nuclear Studies. Fermi saw that as a place where he could build a center for his kind of physics, even as he had in Rome 20 years earlier. Fermi had all sorts of research he wanted to do with the powerful neutron source available from the CP-3 pile at nearby Argonne National Laboratory. And, in common with all nuclear physicists, he was eager to explore the internal workings of atomic nuclei by building accelerators of ever-higher energy.

Fermi could have headed the new Institute, if he had wanted, but he was wise enough to leave the administration to Sam Allison, who had been at his side both for the work on the Chicago pile and at Los Alamos. Fermi attracted other stars to the new Institute and to the physics department at the University of Chicago. Edward Teller, of the "Super" hydrogen bomb, came. Herbert Anderson, who had been Fermi's student at Columbia and teammate at CP-1 and Los Alamos, joined the faculty of the University, as did Leona Marshall, the one woman present when the Chicago pile had gone critical.

Younger men (they were almost all men in those days) who had worked in the Manhattan Project and knew Fermi's great reputation came to Chicago, too. People who were graduate students and postdoctoral fellows then, went on to distinguished careers and—some of them—to Nobel Prizes of their own.

Fermi liked being among young people. He would have lunch with his students, and he instituted seminars like those he had run in Italy. Thoroughly Americanized after six

Throughout his career, Fermi kept a blackboard in his office for teaching and sharing theoretical insights with colleagues.

intense years in the United States, he cheerfully joined in the games, dances, and hikes that were so much a part of university life. And the Fermis' new home near the university was often a stopping place for their many scientist friends.

But all was not fun and games. There were many new issues to think through and debate. The new field of atomic energy required new laws for its regulation. One major issue was civilian versus military control of atomic energy. Another was the issue of secrecy; Fermi wanted a maximum of free communication. No one wanted to give away the details of how to make an atomic bomb, but free discussion of basic nuclear physics would help that science advance.

It was the issue of civilian versus military control that gave scientists their first opportunity to learn the art of lobbying, of influencing lawmakers in Congress. A bill was being put through Congress called the May-Johnson bill. That bill had been drafted with lots of input from the War Department and very little from scientists. It gave the military a major role in the development of atomic energy in all forms, not just weapons. Many—indeed, most—scientists were opposed to that. They wanted civilian control to ensure lots of attention to basic research and peaceful uses of atomic energy. That would be in keeping with the American tradition of having civilians at the very top of the military services.

The scientists, with those from the former Metallurgical Laboratory in the lead, lobbied in support of an alternative bill, the MacMahon bill. Many months of hearings and debate followed, and in the end, a modified form of civilian control won out. A U.S. Atomic Energy Commission (AEC) was established to take over the facilities and responsibilities of the army and its Manhattan Engineering District. Interestingly, Fermi had supported the May-Johnson bill with its military control. In fact, he had joined with Oppenheimer and E. O. Lawrence, another giant of the wartime effort, to plead for May-Johnson. (Fermi's principal concern was that they not slow the development of atomic energy. It turned out to be an unnecessary concern, in part because Fermi was made a member of the advisory setup in the new civilian-controlled AEC.)

The new Atomic Energy Commission had a General Advisory Committee (GAC) of scientists and engineers. Oppenheimer was chairman of the first such GAC, and Fermi was one of its eight members. It was a position Fermi probably would have preferred *not* to have, but this Italian immigrant, so successfully re-established in the United States, had a strong sense of duty. During his five-year term as a member of the GAC, Fermi made many trips to Washington to share in advising the AEC. He and his fellow advisors dealt with issues very important to the security and safety of his adopted country. Indeed, many of them were important to the future of all of humanity because they dealt with the control of atomic weapons.

In late October 1949, the General Advisory Committee took up the question of whether to start a crash effort to develop a hydrogen bomb. By then the Russians had exploded their first atomic bomb, ending the American monopoly. Unfortunately, Russia and the United States had gone from being wartime allies to being cold-war enemies. Nonetheless, the GAC recommended that no crash H-bomb effort be started. They felt that would endanger the ongoing effort to perfect and stockpile fission-based A-bombs.

Furthermore, Fermi and I. I. Rabi (another scientist member of the advisory committee) argued, hydrogen bombs, if they could be made, could be made powerful without limit, and ". . . we think it is wrong on fundamental ethical principles to initiate the development of such a weapon." Despite the opinion of those experts, on January 31, 1950, President Harry Truman ordered work on the hydrogen bomb to proceed. Fear of the Russians made the political pressure for a go-ahead irresistible.

Many other issues came before the GAC. To all of them, Fermi brought his intelligence, conscientiousness, and strong sense of duty. That pattern is now well established as

The General Advisory Committee of the Atomic Energy Commission in 1947 included (left to right) James Conant, Robert Oppenheimer, General James McCormack, Hartley Rowe, John Manley, I. I. Rabi, and Roger Werner.

citizens with special competence are called on to advise their government. He would have preferred not to leave his seminars and students in Chicago for those trips to Washington, but America had provided him with refuge. He, his wife, and his children were now citizens. He would be excellent as an advisor as in all other things he did.

And Fermi did bring excellence to his two new posts in Chicago. First, Fermi was a full Professor of Physics at the University of Chicago. With that hat on, he taught classes in physics, conducted seminars, and supervised graduate students, both experimentalists and theoreticians. In his teaching role, Fermi was famous for the clarity of his lectures. He prepared carefully for those classes. One of his students, one of those who went on to win a Nobel Prize, remembers: "The discussions were kept at an elementary level. The emphasis was always on the essential and the practical part of the topic. . . . We learned that *that* was physics."

Fermi's second post was at the Institute for Nuclear Studies, a research institute. There Fermi could create new theories and design advanced experiments in nuclear physics, using his rare combination of both theoretical and experimental skills. For the theorist in him, there was the inevitable blackboard on which he wrote out equations or clarified a calculation for a visitor. But he also had a well-equipped shop set up next door to his office so that the experimentalist in him could continue his practice of turning out small items needed for an experiment.

He returned to his first love, neutron physics. Now he had the advantage of neutron sources far more powerful than those weak polonium-beryllium sources he had used in Rome. An hour's drive from Chicago, in Lemont, Illinois, was the new Argonne National Laboratory. A more advanced version of the original Chicago Pile-1 had been built there. For the moderator, it used heavy water. Heavy water is water in which the hydrogen atoms of H_2O had been replaced by the heavy isotope H^2, also called deuterium. (The hydrogen atom has a single proton as its nucleus; heavy hydrogen has a proton and a neutron in its nucleus and a reduced tendency to absorb neutrons—that makes heavy water a better moderator in a pile.) There was also a "thermal column" of graphite from which a beam of neutrons could be accessed.

Leona Wood Marshall worked with Fermi at the University of Chicago, Hanford, and the Argonne National Laboratory.

In her comments on these postwar neutron researches, Fermi's collaborator, Leona Marshall, shares Fermi's philosophy of experimentation:

> any straightforward measurement . . . where there is a promising ignorance. The attempt to understand the results should in turn suggest new measurements. In his collaboration, we felt his sweet reasonableness, steady competence with situations he could influence, and restrained amusement at frustrations beyond his control.

This seems to be a good philosophy for many aspects of life.

With this strong source of neutrons, Fermi could study the properties of different materials at selected neutron energies. He had two different ways to select neutrons of a particular energy. Those two very different methods are a beautiful illustration of the two ways physics gives us to describe neutrons issuing from a pile. One way is to see them as a stream of particles; the other is to see them as a mixture of waves.

The particle approach separates neutrons according to their speed, using what is called a velocity selector. A velocity selector makes use of a revolving shutter consisting of thin foils of neutron-absorbing cadmium alternating with thin sheets of aluminum that can readily transmit neutrons. As it rotates, the shutter is "open," with no cadmium in the way, for just a brief period of time, letting a burst of neu-

A cross section of the shutter of the velocity selector. The Shutter rotates around an axis perpendicular to the page; only in the position shown can a burst of neutrons avoid capture in cadmium absorbers and streak down in the direction shown.

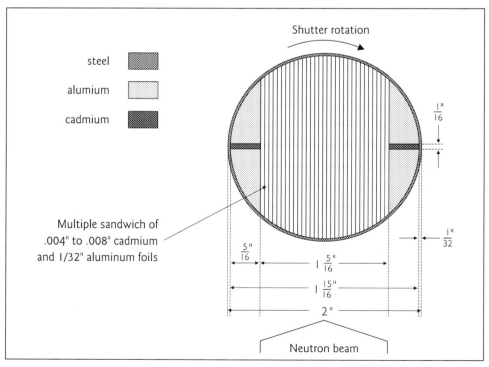

trons go through. As that burst moves, the faster neutrons get ahead of the slower ones, and the neutrons spread out in space according to their velocities. They move toward detectors a known distance away, with an absorbing or scattering target in the path. Electronic circuits of no great complexity activate the neutron-detecting apparatus when the neutrons traveling at a selected speed arrive at the detectors. This way the experimenters count only the neutrons that were moving at the right velocity to get from the shutter to the target in the desired time (and then on to the detectors).

The second method for selecting neutrons of a particular energy is to take advantage of their wavelike properties. In the world of the atom, where quantum mechanics applies rather than Newton's mechanics of our everyday experience, neutrons can behave as waves. Neutrons can be separated according to their wavelength just as light passing through a prism is separated into its spectrum of colors. Fermi used crystals of calcium fluoride (CaF_2) and other materials to select neutrons of a particular wavelength (and therefore a particular, single energy). By adjusting the angle at which the neutrons were reflected from the crystal, Fermi could study the absorption of neutrons in target materials as the neutron energy was varied. And that, in turn, gave insights into the structure of the nucleus.

Fermi did a beautiful series of experiments in which he reflected a single-energy beam off another crystal. Doing this enabled him to learn important information about something called the "scattering length" of the elements in that second crystal. He also did experiments in which he simply reflected his neutron beam off a polished mirror, just as light might have been reflected. Think of it as neutron optics.

It is a lovely illustration of the unity of physics and the wholeness of Fermi's approach that there can be mirrors for neutrons just as there are for light. In the same way, Fermi borrowed techniques and theory developed for studying the way X-rays are bent by crystals and applied them to neu-trons. A wave is a wave is a wave, in the hands of a complete physicist such as Fermi.

Fermi's feel for the unity of physics was further evident in a new phase of his researches. Starting in 1947, there were new particles and new concerns in Fermi's published papers. Terms such as "mesons" and "pions" and titles such as "Are Mesons Elementary Particles?" begin to dominate his publications. That reflects a postwar surge in interest in what held a nucleus together. After all, the protons inside a nucleus, being positively charged, ought to repel each other and fly apart. There was another force—a specifically nuclear force—that held them all together with their neigh-boring neutrons.

The term meson means middle particle. These are parti-cles a few hundred times heavier than an electron yet only a fifth or so the mass of a proton or neutron. So they are in the middle in terms of their mass. It later turned out that there was a veritable zoo of such particles, but the one that occu-pied Fermi's attention in 1947 and for the next few years were the pi-mesons or pions. A particle of that kind had been suggested by a Japanese physicist named Yukawa as the source of the nuclear force. Fermi himself explained (in a popular talk he gave in 1952) about mesons and nuclear forces:

> According to Yukawa theory, a neutron will occasionally convert into a proton plus a pi-meson, which will then be reabsorbed and thrown out again and reabsorbed and so on. The nuclear field involved in this . . . odd ball game requires an amount of energy . . . Who pays for this amount of energy? Well, nobody; so if nobody pays one has to bor-row. Now in this bank of energy there is a very special rule, namely, the larger the loan the shorter the term.

Fermi goes on to explain how quantum mechanics sets the duration of the "loan" and therefore the distance a meson can dart out of the neutron before having to be reabsorbed. From that line of reasoning came a value for the

Enrico Fermi (far left) with Emilio Segrè, Hideki Yukawa, and Gian Carlo Wick in Berkeley, California, in 1948.

mass of the pi-meson that was at least in range with what began to be observed when accelerators were developed that were powerful enough to make pi-mesons observable in the laboratory.

Evidence of these new members of the nuclear fraternity had also come from studies of cosmic rays, the particles and superhigh-energy radiation that rain down on Earth from outer space. Physicists had sent counters up in balloons and set up labs on mountaintops to study those cosmic rays. Even when their counters were shielded by many thick plates of lead, there were rays that got through. What were these particles? Where did they come from? And what relation did they bear to these theories that every nucleus was held together by particles that shuttled back and forth between the nucleons?

That was the postwar preoccupation of many physicists, now free from their wartime weapons work. They now had the resources to support their habits, their addiction to investigation. At university after university, accelerators were built that could push protons or electrons to energies a hundred times greater than before the war. These machines were called betatrons, synchrotrons, or even synchrocyclotrons, and the design and construction of such machines was a major new field of physics and engineering.

Fermi's Institute for Nuclear Studies was among them. Their machine was to accelerate protons to energies equivalent to that you would reach if you had a battery rated at 450 million volts and used it to push a proton from one terminal to the other. Except it was not a battery; all these accelerators involved sending particles around and around in a circular path, increasing their energy further with each circuit.

Fermi brought to this new machine his sharp sense of where the most critical experiments lay. The unity of physics, the fact that a few simple principles underlie all the surface complexity, served him well. It meant he could do with these very high-energy pions what he had done with his low-energy neutrons. While the details of experiments such as "Total Cross Section of Negative Pions in Hydrogen" are beyond the scope of this book, the title alone makes clear that Fermi was, as always, looking at a simple example (hydrogen, the lightest element) and was using a technique (scattering) that he could milk thoroughly for the insights it would provide.

Fermi explained the scattering technique in that popular talk he gave, saying:

> One hurls [a pi-meson at a proton] and sees how they are deflected. From the features of the deflection, the angular distribution, the energy dependence, and so on, one hopes to deduce the force responsible for the deflection.

In the years that followed that Total Cross Section paper, Fermi published increasingly sophisticated studies of pion scattering. His experiments and piercing analysis of the results of those experiments enabled physicists to eliminate at least some of the many competing theories of nuclear forces then popular.

Fermi's handiness as an experimenter shows up nicely in something that came to be called Fermi's Trolley. The pions for his scattering experiments were generated when protons, accelerated to high energy in their cyclotron, struck a target. To get pions of a different energy, it was necessary to move the target, a move that would be clumsy indeed if you had to shut down the machine, lose the vacuum in the accelerator, adjust the target, and then fire up the machine once again. Fermi designed this little cart to hold his targets; its wheels ran on the surface of the lower pole of the huge magnet that guided the protons in their circular orbits. Fermi recognized that he could create a motor by using the magnetic field of the cyclotron together with current he would send through a small coil mounted on the cart. That would move the cart remotely, as needed. The Fermi Trolley is not the stuff of Nobel Prizes, but it shows Fermi's taste for the simple, the ingenious, the direct.

Important as they were, pion experiments did not occupy all of Fermi's time. He published a total of 25 papers in the next few years. They reflect, as always, his wide-ranging interests. His mind reached out into space, with papers on the way in which magnetic fields in space could accelerate cosmic rays to their very high energies. And his mind reached out to the future in studies of what might be done with electronic computers, then just coming into full use.

Fermi spent the summer of 1953 at Los Alamos, using their MANIAC electronic computer to analyze the results of the experiments he had conducted on pion scattering. He also pioneered the use of electronic computers to simulate simple experiments and to get a feel for the solution of what are called nonlinear problems—problems for which there were no direct mathematical solutions. In 1953 Fermi was also elected president of the American Physical Society, the principal organization of physicists in the United States. That was yet another measure of the extent to which he had entered fully into the life of his adopted country.

Part of his motivation was that scientists were under attack. The United States was obsessed with concerns about security risks and communist influence in government—concerns largely exaggerated and spurred for political ends by the likes of Wisconsin's Senator Joseph McCarthy. In that semi-hysterical climate, J. Robert Oppenheimer, who had led the successful development of

Fermi used the MANIAC computer at Los Alamos to interpret the data from his pion-scattering experiments. Built there in 1952, it was slow by modern standards but proved far superior to the mechanical calculators used in wartime.

the atomic bomb at Los Alamos, was accused of spying for the Russians from 1936 to 1942. Lewis Strauss, newly appointed to head the AEC, announced that Oppenheimer's security clearance would be suspended pending an investigation. Oppenheimer had been a hero, an almost mythic figure in the world of physics. His talents as a theorist and an administrator had led to the weapon that ended the war. Yet there were those determined to cast doubt on his reliability and "loyalty."

Hearings were held in the spring of 1954. More than 40 witnesses testified. Fermi's testimony supported Oppenheimer; they had shared many decisions as fellow members of the General Advisory Committee of the AEC. Fermi could attest to the soundness of Oppenheimer's recommendations. But there were others who—more with innuendo than with facts—cast doubt on the loyalty of the man who had run Los Alamos. Oppenheimer was stripped of his security clearance.

Problems of a different sort now arose to plague Fermi. Clearly, he could have gone on to scale still more heights of service and science. But it was not to be. Cancer was spreading within his body even as he continued his researches in the spring of 1954.

Enrico Fermi relaxing off Isola d'Elba, Italy, in 1954, the year of his death. Ever devoted to physics, he had given advanced courses while in Italy and France that summer.

A Great Man Honored and Remembered

In the summer of 1954, Fermi went to Europe and lectured on pion scattering at an advanced summer school conducted by the Italian Physical Society at beautiful Lake Como. Fermi wanted to hike in the surrounding countryside, as he had so often in the past. But he lacked his usual energy. Something was wrong.

When he returned to Chicago, the source of his illness became tragically clear: an exploratory operation revealed that Fermi had cancer, a particularly insidious form that had spread to several parts of his body. It was a hopeless case. The death of this great man lay only weeks ahead.

The news of Fermi's fatal illness spread quickly throughout the scientific world. In his biography of Fermi, *Enrico Fermi, Physicist,* Emilio Segrè relates how the word reached him:

> I had just returned from a trip to South America when I received a telephone call from Sam Allison, who, in a broken, almost unintelligible voice, told me of the operation that had been performed that morning and its result. I did not know that Fermi had not been well, but the tone of Allison's voice instantly revealed the truth. I went to Chicago as soon as possible.

Fermi was resting in the hospital, with his wife in attendance, and was being fed [intravenously]. In typical fashion, he was measuring the flux of the nutrient by counting drops and timing them with a stopwatch. It seemed as if he were performing one of his usual physics experiments on an extraneous object.

Segrè had been among Fermi's very first student in Rome. One of his most recent students in Chicago, C. N. Yang, paid a similar visit to the hospital. Here is what he wrote:

Fermi fell critically ill in the fall of 1954. Murray Gell-Mann [a fellow physicist], who was then at Columbia University, and I went to Chicago to see him in Billings Hospital. As we entered his room, he was reading a book which was a collection of stories about men who by their willpower succeeded in overcoming fantastic natural obstacles and misfortunes. He was very thin, but only a little sad. He told us very calmly about his condition: The doctors had said that in a few days he might go home, but that he would not have more than months to live. He then showed us the notebook by his bedside, and said that it was his own notebook on nuclear physics. He planned, when he left the hospital, in the two months' time left, to revise it for publication. Gell-Mann and I were so overwhelmed by his simple determination and his devotion to physics, that we were afraid for a few moments to look into his face. (Fermi died within three weeks of our visit.)

On November 16, 1954, with his death imminent, Fermi was named as the recipient of a special $25,000 award from the Atomic Energy Commission for his achievements. President Dwight Eisenhower had "enthusiastically approved" the recommendation of Lewis Strauss, Chairman of the AEC, to honor Fermi in this special way.

Fermi died on November 29, 1954. His gravestone reads, simply, and very appropriately,

Enrico Fermi
1901–1954
Physicist

More than any physicist of our time, Fermi's name and works live on. The most substantial monument is the great Fermi National Accelerator Laboratory or Fermilab, 35 miles west of Chicago. There a giant accelerator probes, as Fermi had, for understanding.

Other honors have followed. The Institute for Nuclear Studies, which Fermi had helped found after he left Los Alamos, was renamed in his honor, the Enrico Fermi Institute. The Italian Physical Society's summer school, where Fermi taught the last summer of his life, is now named for him.

In 1955, the year after Fermi's death, the radioactive element with atomic number 100 was named Fermium in his honor. It is fitting that the element named in his honor follows Einsteinium, named in honor of Albert Einstein. Fermi's name is also emblazoned across much of physics because of theories he created. First among these is surely Fermi-Dirac statistics. Phenomena from the way electrons move in metals to the way the electrons in an atom behave can be explained with the use of Fermi's theory.

The universe is full of matter that consists mainly of electrons, neutrons, and protons; therefore the universe is filled with fermions. That is a nice tribute to this great man, whose mind encompassed so much understanding of the physics of so much of the universe.

On the fiftieth anniversary of the first nuclear chain reaction, scientists who had worked with Fermi over the

Fermilab, the Fermi National Accelerator Laboratory in Batavia, Illinois.

years gathered at the University of Chicago for a commemorative meeting. Former students and colleagues of Fermi shared their memories of him.

Speaker after speaker referred to Fermi's special qualities as a teacher. One, for example, said, "He so enjoyed the act of teaching. He enjoyed students who did not immediately grasp his point because he could repeat his explanation and thereby double his pleasure." Another spoke of a central lesson learned: "You work everything out, you never delude yourself by thinking you probably could do something if only you wanted to; you do it and you write it down so you can recover it when necessary." And a third remembered, "Fermi's talent for concentrating on your problem made it a pleasure to be his colleague."

They were equally high in praise of his personal qualities, pointing to his modesty, his reserve, his dislike of pretension of whatever kind, and how he did not like to "throw his weight around." "Fermi was a kind and brilliant friend . . . a wonderful person who made physics an exciting experience," was the way one colleague put it.

They also reminded each other, this gathering of friends and ex-students did, of his competitive spirit; "He liked to win," said one. He also prided himself on his physical stamina and would shame his students into extended exposure to a brutally cold Lake Michigan.

Fermi was a man of great and extraordinarily focused intellect. His great energy enabled him to set and maintain high standards in his work. He was highly competitive by nature, but expended that in athletics, leaving a residue of helpfulness and agreeableness. As a teacher and as a colleague, he was generous, ever willing to share from his great store of knowledge and scientific instinct. Combining great talent in both theory and experiment with an almost animal zest for "doing" physics, he was unmatched in his time.

After his death, the award the AEC had inaugurated by giving the first such prize to Fermi was renamed the Fermi

Prize in his honor. It is given each year to "recognize someone of international esteem whose career has been marked by continued exceptional contribution to the development, use, or control of nuclear energy." Some of the most distinguished scientists of our age have been honored in this way. (The Fermi Prize for 1963 was awarded to J. Robert Oppenheimer. It was a way for the government to make amends for what had clearly been a miscarriage of justice in a time of hysteria.) By coincidence, the winner for 1995 was Ugo Fano, Fermi's last student in Italy, and among the award winners in 1996 (there were three that year) was Richard Garwin, one of Fermi's most brilliant students at the University of Chicago. To keep up with inflation, the cash award had been increased to $100,000 by then.

J. Robert Oppenheimer receiving the Atomic Energy Commission's first Fermi Award from President Lyndon Johnson in December 1963, a belated attempt to make up for the unfair security charges against the wartime director of Los Alamos.

One of the objectives of the Fermi Award is "To inspire people of all ages through the example of Enrico Fermi . . . and the Fermi Award laureates who have continued in his tradition."

While Fermi Statistics, his mastery of neutron physics, the neutrino, and his theory of beta decay may be the accomplishments for which his fellow scientists honor him, it is the creation of the world's first controlled nuclear chain reaction that most affects the average person today. It led to a weapon of unprecedented power: the plutonium bomb, but it also led to a new source of electrical energy, radioisotopes for medical diagnosis and healing, and powerful sources of neutrons for research in many fields. And then there is his example as a human being: supremely bright, energetic, conscientious, disciplined, using his great mental powers to wrest more understanding of how the physical world works, for above all, he was a physicist.

CHRONOLOGY

1901
Enrico Fermi born on September 29, the third child of Alberto Fermi and Ida De Gattis

1911
Enters *ginnasio* (middle school)

1914
Meets father's friend, Adolfo Amidei, who becomes his mentor

1915
Brother Giulio dies at age 15; makes lifetime friend of schoolmate Enrico Persico

1918
Gains admission to the Scuola Normale Superiore in Pisa. Also enrolls at the university there

1921
Publishes first scientific paper

1922
Earns Ph.D. from University of Pisa

1923
Uses postdoctoral fellowship to study at University of Göttingen, Germany

1924
Teaching assistant at University of Rome; mother dies on May 8; goes to Leyden, The Netherlands, on a three-month fellowship

1925
Joins Franco Rasetti at the University of Florence; does first experimental work

1926
Creates theory of Fermi statistics; wins the new chair of theoretical physics at University of Rome

1927

Joined in Rome by Rasetti; uses statistical approach for rough, but useful, theory of atoms

1928

Marries Laura Capon, July 19

1929

Appointed by Mussolini to the Italian Academy

1930

Summers at University of Michigan, Ann Arbor, his first visit to United States; resolves to focus on nuclear physics

1933

Explains beta decay, using neutrino to maintain energy conservation

1934

Experiments on inducing radioactivity by irradiating with neutrons begin; uses paraffin rather than lead, demonstrating slow-neutron effects

1935

Fission missed by Fermi team because aluminum foil covers uranium target; Italian patent on slow-neutron method of inducing radioactivity

1938

Anti-Semitic racial laws promulgated by Italians influence Fermi's resolve to leave Italy; wins Nobel Prize in physics; Fission detected by Hahn and Strassmann, interpreted by Frisch and Meitner

1939

Arrives in New York with his family; starts research on fission, chain reaction at Columbia with colleagues

1941

Japanese bomb Pearl Harbor, Hawaii, on December 7;

United States enters World War II the next day

1942

Moves pile research to Chicago; produces first-ever sustained chain reaction on December 2

1943

Attends planning conferences at Los Alamos

1944

Construction completed on Hanford production reactors; moves full-time to Los Alamos

1945

First atomic bomb tested at Alamogordo, New Mexico; atomic bombs dropped on Hiroshima and Nagasaki, Japan

1946

Returns to University of Chicago; joins new Institute for Nuclear Studies

1947

Appointed to General Advisory Committee of Atomic Energy Commission

1951

Begins high-energy pion experiments with new Chicago cyclotron

1953

Becomes president of the American Physical Society

1954

Testifies on behalf of J. Robert Oppenheimer at security hearing; Fermi dies of cancer on November 29

Biographies of Fermi

Fermi, Enrico. *Collected Papers, Volumes I and II.* Chicago: University of Chicago Press, 1962 and 1965. These two volumes contain all of Fermi's published works along with many comments by his collaborators that provide rewarding insights into the man and his work.

Fermi, Laura. *Atoms in the Family.* Chicago: University of Chicago Press, 1954. Fermi's wife wrote this charming account of his work and their life together.

Segrè, Emilio. *Enrico Fermi, Physicist.* Chicago: University of Chicago Press, 1970. By Fermi's student, friend, and fellow Nobel Prize winner.

Accounts of the Atomic Bomb Project

Compton, Arthur Holly. *Atomic Quest.* New York: Oxford University Press, 1956.

Conant, James Bryant. *My Several Lives.* New York: Harper & Row, 1970.

Davis, Nuell Pharr. *Lawrence & Oppenheimer.* New York: Simon & Schuster, 1968.

Fermi, Rachel, and Esther Samra. *Picturing the Bomb.* New York: Harry N. Abrams, 1995. Fermi's granddaughter, Rachel, is co-author of a book of photographs that bring the Manhattan Project to life.

Groves, Leslie. *Now It Can Be Told.* New York: Harper & Row, 1962.

Hewlett, Richard G., and Oscar E. Anderson, Jr. *The New World, 1939/1946.* University Park: Pennsylvania State University Press, 1962. This is the Atomic Energy Commission's history of the wartime atomic program.

Libby, Leona Marshall. *The Uranium People.* New York: Charles Scribner's Sons, 1979.

Rhodes, Richard. *The Making of the Atomic Bomb.* New York: Simon & Schuster, 1986. The definitive account of the A-bomb effort, deserving winner of a Pulitzer Prize.

Sachs, Robert G., ed. *The Nuclear Chain Reaction—Forty Years Later.* Chicago: University of Chicago Press, 1984. Fermi's colleagues gathered in Chicago in 1982 to reflect on the atom; these are the proceedings.

Serber, Robert. *The Los Alamos Primer.* Berkeley: University of California Press, 1992. The once supersecret lectures to newly recruited scientists on how A-bombs are supposed to work.

Szilard, Leo. *Leo Szilard, His Version of the Facts.* Edited by Spencer R. Weart and Gertrude Weiss Szilard. Cambridge, Mass.: MIT Press, 1978. (Paperback edition, 1980). Szilard, who first conceived of a neutron chain reaction, is too special a thinker and writer to miss.

Teller, Edward. *The Legacy of Hiroshima.* New York: Doubleday, 1962.

The Politics of Atom Bombs

Smith, Alice Kimball. *A Peril and a Hope.* Cambridge, Mass.: MIT Press, 1971. The postwar political efforts of atomic scientists are thoroughly covered here.

U.S. Atomic Energy Commission. *In the Matter of J. Robert Oppenheimer.* Cambridge, Mass.: MIT Press, 1971. In a tragic miscarriage of justice, Oppenheimer's security clearance was removed.

The Lighter Side of Los Alamos

Feynman, Richard. *Surely You're Joking, Mr. Feynman.* New York: W. W. Norton, 1985. The funniest person at Los Alamos wrote this book.

Web Sites and Tours

To see the very impressive state of nuclear research today consult the web sites for Los Alamos National Laboratory, Argonne National Laboratory, or Fermi National Accelerator Laboratory (Fermilab) at their respective web sites: *www.lanl.gov*, *www.anl.gov*, and *www.fnal.gov*. All three laboratories give on-site tours.

ACKNOWLEDGMENTS

I owe special thanks to Professor Albert Wattenberg of the Physics Department, University of Illinois in Urbana- Champaign, Illinois, who worked alongside Enrico Fermi at Columbia University and then in the construction of CP-1 at the Metallurgical Laboratory in Chicago. He has been a generous supplier of his own papers on Fermi and on CP-1. Jim Dutton of Argonne National Laboratory helped with material from the 50th anniversary celebration of that first reactor.

The librarians of the public library serving my hometown of South Orange, New Jersey, have been indispensable, especially Ms. Nancy Janow, who made trip after trip to bring me relevant books. Irwin Genzer, head of the science department at our Columbia High School and Lee Kornhauser of the South Orange Middle School provided useful insights into the interests of their students. My sister, Anita Smith, helped in mining Laura Fermi's affectionate biography of her husband, Enrico. Gene Dannen, biographer of Leo Szilard, provided a helpful review of Chapter 4 and the example of his own diligence.

From Los Alamos National Laboratory, John Gustavson of the Public Information Office and Roger Meade, archivist, were particularly helpful in providing background on the stirring days when the atomic bomb was developed there. Professor Philip Morrison of MIT also provided helpful anecdotal material. Christine Baudino, widow of Fermi's bodyguard, John Baudino, generously shared material from his scrapbooks as well as her own reminiscences of Los Alamos.

Rachel Fermi, granddaughter of Enrico Fermi and herself the author of a photographic history of the atom-bomb project, has been a source of encouragement and of leads to visual resources. Judith Neale helped me access the wonderful songs her physicist/father, Arthur Roberts, wrote some 50 years ago.

Owen Gingerich, General Editor of this series, showed exquisite timing by proposing I write this book when I needed a lift and a new direction. He also exposed me to the rigor of his example as a historian of science. Anna Eberhardt, Editorial Assistant at Oxford University Press, helped by translating correspondence with Italian sources. Nancy Toff, my editor at Oxford University Press, provided encouragement and insightful suggestions that make this book serve you—its readers—better.

Finally I thank Maggie Constan for her affectionate support and example of ever-replenishing energy.

PICTURE CREDITS

Dan Cooper earned his Ph.D. in nuclear physics at Massachusetts Institute of Technology. He has served as managing editor of *Nucleonics*, as excutive editor and then publisher of *International Science & Technology*, and is currently president of Cooper Communications, which specializes in science writing. Dr. Cooper once had the great pleasure of hearing Enrico Fermi lecture on the future of particle accelerators.

Owen Gingerich is Professor of Astronomy and of the History of Science at the Harvard-Smithsonian Center for Astrophysics in Cambridge, Massachusetts. The author of more than 400 articles and reviews, he has also written *The Great Copernicus Chase and Other Adventures in Astronomical History* and *The Eye of Heaven: Ptolomy, Copernicus, Kepler.*